I0155514

Get some free, tasty goodies,

even if you don't buy this book!

Your Book Bakery

OPEN

www.harshmanservices.com/ybb-book-goodies

Praise for *Your Book Bakery: Making it easy to write a book*

Jennifer was the right chef in the kitchen to take my manuscript from a hodgepodge of ingredients to a complete product of pure decadence and delight! I wish I had met her before beginning to write my first book, but she'll certainly be receiving my future creations from the absolute jump! She has that special leavening that gives rise to a well-crafted and finished product that helps a writer confidently bring their visions of a nonfiction book from ideation to masterfully presented goodness!

Starting with the right recipe for success is critical for the work you'll put into creating your end result. The front-end effort is worth the long-term reward. Make it easier on yourself when writing your book, and grab the right tool for the job!

—Ken Hannaman,
author of *Ungraduated: Finding your why and dropping out of outdated belief systems*

Jennifer Harshman has written a guide that takes the cake on how to write a nonfiction book. I am currently following the methods outlined in *Your Book Bakery: Making it easy to write a book* for my first self-help book. I have found the steps beneficial in creating a solid manuscript. As someone who typically writes fiction, I needed help figuring out how to get my nonfiction idea on paper. *Your Book Bakery* does exactly that, in bite-sized, orderly steps. I highly recommend this book to anyone who has a desire to write a book but no idea where to start. Bravo, Jennifer. You've created a recipe that will work in every kitchen.

—Tammy Arlene,
author of *From Pain to Purpose*

I often refer authors to Jennifer Harshman with the simple statement that I trust her. Now it's my honor to recommend her book. It carries the same excellence that comes through in her work. Enjoy baking your book with Jennifer!

—Mike Loomis,
book developer and brand strategist

I've known Jennifer Harshman for years and have seen many of the books she's helped to develop. She's been a guest on my podcast several times and always delivers value no matter what the medium or platform. She's also been the editor for several of my own books as well as books I've written for clients.

In this book, Jennifer lays out the success path for you to write your own book. She calls it a recipe, which is the perfect metaphor. This is the recipe you need to bake your helpful nonfiction book. She takes the fear out of writing a book and makes the process fun and rewarding. My friend Jennifer will be with you every step of the way, and you'll quickly realize that she's your friend, too.

—Kent Sanders,
ghostwriter and host of *The Daily Writer* podcast and founder of The Daily Writer Club
former professor and author of multiple books, including 18 *Words to Live By*, and coauthor of *The Faith of Elvis*

After Jennifer Harshman edited my book, *Legendary: A simple playbook for building and living a legendary life and being remembered as a legend*, I wrote a note inside the cover and sent her a copy. That note expressed my gratitude for her guidance, wisdom, and expertise and ended with, "Here's to building and living a legendary life and leaving this world a better place than we found it. Carpe diem, my fellow beautiful human." Jennifer will help you leave this world a better place than you found it, too, as she helps you write and publish your book. Carpe diem, beautiful humans.

—Tommy Breedlove,
author of *Legendary: A simple playbook for building and living a legendary life and being remembered as a legend*

A book is a powerful way to establish your credibility and authority—and reach a new audience with your message. Don't be intimidated by the process. Everyone has a book in them, and Jennifer's easy-to-follow recipe will be your guide!

—Nick Loper,
Side Hustle Nation founder and host, and author of several books, including *$1000 100 Ways* and *Work Smarter: 500 online resources today's top entrepreneurs use to increase productivity and achieve their goals*

Jennifer asked me if I would be interested in reading her manuscript on writing a book. Little did she know that 1) I have a book ready to be published that's been sitting here for six years. Talk about impostor syndrome, and 2) I did just finish writing a chapter for a book where several of us will be talking about chronic illness. In both cases, I really could have used *Your Book Bakery*. While I don't bake cakes, the concepts behind this are brilliant. I love the whole idea of taking it step by step like baking a cake. I am going back to my original manuscript and reworking it based on the process in this book. It will really help me finally get this together and published.

Thanks, Jennifer, for such an insightful, easy to understand and follow guide to doing something that so many of us want to do but are not sure of how to do it.

—Nancy Becher,

chief flying pig wrangler at Invisible Entrepreneurs

I've heard Jennifer Harshman say that writing a book is a process that can be repeated, and all you need is a recipe to follow and the willingness to take action. This book is an essential guide not only on the ins and outs of writing a great book but also on avoiding the endless pitfalls along the way.

—Vincent Pugliese,

author of *Freelance to Freedom: The roadmap for creating a side business to achieve financial, time, and life freedom* and *The Wealth of Connection: A new approach to making business personal.*

Your Book Bakery:

Making it easy to write a book

Jennifer Harshman

Your Book Bakery: Making it easy to write a book

Copyright © 2010 by Jennifer Harshman

ISBN: 978-1-950721-25-2

All rights reserved. No part of this publication may be reproduced, distributed, or transmitted in any form or by any means, including photocopying, recording, or other electronic or mechanical methods, without the prior written permission, except in the case of brief quotations embodied in critical reviews and certain other noncommercial uses permitted by copyright law.

Harshman House Publishing
P.O.Box 82
Spring Valley, IL 61362
harshmanservices.com

Printed in the United States of America

Ingredients

Foreword by Dan Miller

Jennifer Harshman has come a long way since I first encountered her through my website in 2003, when she was struggling to find a way to live out her purpose. The first live conversation I had with her was about nine years later, during an evening Q&A session with my son Kevin Miller, where we were advising people on their business ideas. I told her on that call that being a freelance editor wasn't the greatest idea. "An editor? Well, I can find an editor anywhere; that's a commodity," I said, not knowing at the time that she was already doing it full-time or that she did far more for her clients than just editing.

Over the years, I got to know Jennifer and her sweet and generous spirit. I watched her add offerings as the number of books she worked on stacked up and up and up. I saw her work and name pop up all over the place. I saw her navigate the ups and downs all entrepreneurs go through and even witnessed her struggles with her health and some family issues. As her mentor, I cheered her on through it all. I made recommendations, and she listened.

Jennifer improved books that became *Wall Street Journal*, *USA Today*, and *New York Times* bestsellers, including one of mine. When it came time for the 2020 edition of my flagship book, *48 Days to the Work (and Life) You Love*, I asked Jennifer if she would edit it. She was thrilled to, and I loved her work.

Hundreds of authors have benefitted directly from Jennifer's help. She coached through the writing process and edited books for people who collectively went on to change millions of lives through their books, blog posts, and speeches. She's helped many of my community members for free or at the 48 Days Eagles discount. That right there is reason enough for anyone to join the 48 Days Eagles!

What's so special about what Jennifer does? Like I said when I first spoke with her, anyone can find an editor, right? As I learned that night and many days since, she's one of a kind, and what she does is extraordinary. She combined the worlds of SEO, writing and editing, and personal productivity to carve out a space all her own and to develop a process you're going to read about in this book.

When you combine your God-given skills, personality traits, values, dreams, and passions, you can create the life and work you love. Many people who have read my books (including the author of this book) have done so.

Jennifer Harshman has long said that writing a book is a replicable process, and that if you know how it's done, you can do it, too. As a multi-published, *New York Times* bestselling author, I couldn't agree more. When she connected writing a book to the concept of following a recipe to bake a cake, everyone who heard "Your Book Bakery" knew exactly what her program (and, later, this book) would be about. It was a hit.

Now you get to taste and see for yourself how sweet it can be to produce a book that will help others. Make a difference as you write your helpful nonfiction book and create the work and life you love.

Dan Miller,

career coach, podcaster, and author of *Write to the Bank, 48 Days to the Work and Life You Love, No More Dreaded Mondays, Wisdom Meets Passion, The Rudder of the Day, An Understanding Heart,* and more

Foreword by John Stange

As the author of more than 30 books so far, I have some experience with authorship. Some of my books have been traditionally published. Others have been self-published. I've hired Jennifer Harshman, The Book Baker, to edit some of my books and invited her to guest post on my blog at DesireJesus.com. I recommend her all the time, and that continues here.

A "content waterfall" is what I call my process of creating and repurposing my content from weekly sermons into blog posts, newsletters, podcast episodes, and books. A content waterfall is a system, a path, a recipe, if you will.

That's what you need to write your book. Jennifer gives you that recipe in this book. If you need additional help, just reach out to her. Nothing lights up her face more than helping people achieve their goals, especially when it comes to writing.

Ask any author what they wish they'd had before they wrote their first book, and they'll most likely tell you they wish they'd had a recipe to follow. They'd want to know exactly how to write their book, for whom, and what to put in it and where. I did everything I've done by trial and error, and it took me several years to reach what I'd call significant success with my content. I know I would have been extremely grateful for such a resource as this one when I was just starting to write books.

Jennifer developed this recipe as she walked many authors through the process of writing their books. Now you have it. Enjoy!

John Stange,

host of several podcasts (*The Chapter a Day Audio Bible* podcast, *Platform Launchers* podcast, *Daily Devotions with Pastor John*, and *Dwell on These Things*)
blogger at DesireJesus.com
author of *Dwell on These Things* and 30+ other books

Preface

In this book, you will find puns, plays on words, metaphors, and silly sayings. You'll also find them in my book-writing program, TikTok channel, and eventual podcast. First off, it's fun. I often say, "Writing is exciting." It doesn't have to be the drudgery we learned to think it is. Also, playing with language in such a way is a sign of high intelligence. For that reason, I'm sure you will enjoy the instances of it in this book.

This entire book is a metaphor: baking is a metaphor for producing your book. I hope you find the process to be quick but measured, uplifting, and so juicy sweet. To help you win, the first thing I want you to do is to get your hands on a baking scent. It might be lemon or cinnamon oil, peppermint, or chocolate. Use it every time you read this book. Then use it every time you write.

You might notice that this book has three parts, like a three-layered cake. I hope that when it's done, the layers aren't too lumpy. I'm doing exactly what I'm asking you to do: produce something imperfect now and perhaps refine it down the road. You can do it, too.

You'll see that I mention many books in this book. As a writing coach, editor, publisher, author, and agency owner (how long is that list?), most of my favorite resources are books. It only makes sense that I'd mention books often. Also, most of the books I mention are a small portion of the books I've edited. The authors worked hard to create tasty morsels for their readers, including you. Please check out those books. Buy and review the ones that appeal to you. See the Resources section.

Remember that what is fun gets done. Bring a spirit of joy to your writing process. Writing is exciting! Some moments will be hard, but it is worth it, and you can do this. I'm here to help you every step of the way.

The Book for You

Many books about writing are theoretical or high-level books. Author, writing podcaster, and former professor Kent Sanders praises me for teaching things that are "extremely practical rather than pie-in-the-sky theory." He says I teach people how to *actually do* the things I talk about. I am thankful for his words because that is my exact intention with everything I do.

You don't need another "anyone can write a book" book. You need a practical path to get it done. That's this book.

This book is a recipe for actually writing your book.

It's for coaches, consultants, subject-matter experts, and other leaders or helpers—even if you haven't started. If you want to write a book that will help others, and if you know your topic well, this is for you—even if you hate writing. You don't have to write your book to write your book. I'll explain that later, I promise.

Those who need to do massive research before writing their book need something other than my 12-week program, but continue to read this book. Email Jennifer@HarshmanServices about a custom package.

Good Enough to Write a Book

Impostor syndrome makes people worry that they're not good enough to write a book. You are good enough to do this. You don't need to know anything about writing a book. We will start from scratch and go through the process together. As long as you have a message you want to share and you keep your promises, this is for you.

Most people can give plenty of reasons why they are not writing as much as they think they should be:

- There's no room in my schedule for writing. I don't have time to write.

- It's hard and complicated.
- Shiny objects lure me away every time.
- Netflix is too tempting, and I just have to binge watch ___.
- Too many other important things crowd it out, and then I'm too tired.

Most blame others, their environment, job, or perceived difficulty of the task. Some accept responsibility in a way that would make my friend John G. Miller smile.

I respect them.

John's the author of *QBQ! The Question Behind the Question*, a book about personal accountability. Their list of reasons/excuses might look like this:

- I overschedule myself and don't prioritize writing.
- I don't know what to do.
- I allow shiny objects to distract me.
- I choose to binge watch instead of write.
- I don't make time for writing, and then I tell myself I'm too tired to write.

You've heard people say, "I have some good news and some bad news." Well, you are going to have to change some behavior if you want to achieve your goals and write your book.

The good news is I can help you do that. The *great news* is it does not have to be torture. In fact, it can be a lot of fun. You might get hooked on writing. You might even decide to join one of my group-coaching programs, and we'll become buddies. Sound like fun?

Start with this book.

Part One
Selecting the Recipe:
Determining which kind

Chapter 1: To Bake or Not to Bake . . .

Writing, to many people, seems complicated and difficult. It's like some secret code that's uncrackable for mere mortals. I'm here to tell you it's not. At least, it's not with nonfiction. Other people think writing a book is like some kind of mystical and mysterious sorcery only a few people can do. The talented wave their wand, and poof! There sits a gorgeous paperback. The people who are wishing they could do it but believing they can't often think it's supernatural. It's not. At least, it's not with nonfiction.

Writing a book is more like following plans to make a birdhouse or following a recipe to make a cake. That's the metaphor used in this book, my coaching program, and my TikTok channel where I share tips and have videos on a few other types of things. Handle: @Jennifer_Harshman.

Every time I started to tell someone the name of the program, halfway through it, they jumped in. "I love the name!" The next sentence was either, "It tells you exactly what you're getting!" or, "It says writing a book is as simple and straightforward as baking a cake. Just follow a recipe and boom, you have a book."

That's exactly what I want to convey.

The concept of "baking a book" is simple, clear, and instantly understood. People understand that it involves following a recipe and getting a finished product. It is simple and straightforward.

Can a book be as intricate as a 7-tier wedding cake? It can, but that's not the kind of book I encourage you (or anyone else) to write. It can be as simple as one very narrow topic, and as short as 2,500 words—a healthy blog post!

Can the book you bake be different from other authors' books? Of course! You're adding some different ingredients than they are.

The flavor could be quite different from other people's products. But it's the same product (a cake and not a coffee table).

Writing a book is a replicable process. Once you have the instructions or the recipe, all you have to do is gather the ingredients and put in the work.

I'm going to give you the recipe and a list of ingredients you get to choose from.

Putting in the work is up to you. But you don't have to do it alone if going it alone is too hard. That's what the group-coaching program is for.

What you need

First, you have to have the right mindset. If you don't, address that and get your chef's hat on straight.

Jeff Goins often says, "You are a writer, so start acting like one."

Now, I'm not saying you need to live in coffee shops, wear Beatnik clothes and a beret, or chain smoke. Nor am I saying stay up all night, bang on the keys, and burn the candle at both ends. You need not adopt any stereotypes of "writer."

The Sifting or the Eggs

Which came first, the sifting or the eggs? The group-coaching program came before this book did. I hadn't planned to write this book. I had already written a manual for Your Book Bakery. But several people asked me to write a full book to go with it.

So I did.

You're a professional. Whether you work at home, go to an office, or anything else, you dress decently. You try to take care of yourself, too.

I'm not even going to say you have to be a writer. You don't have to consider yourself a writer to be an author. Being a writer is more a permanent state of ongoing action than being an author is.

To pull this off and write a book or populate your blog with posts, you'll need to set up your environment for your success.

That includes the following:

- your physical environment such as your desk
- the amount of solitude/companionship you need
- your electronic environment such as your computer files and calendar
- your temporal environment such as your schedule
- your mental environment such as the self-talk and thinking you indulge in

My motto

With the right attitude and resources, you can do amazing things, and if you choose the first, you *will* find the second.

You are about to set forth on a journey (or maybe you've already started it and gotten stuck) where you are the hero on a quest.

I'm your guide. I've helped hundreds of people make it to the mountaintop, and I'll help you, too, if you want it.

Are you ready to find out whether you should write a book and why? Do you want to know how to get your book written and out into the world where it can do these things?

- serve others who might become your clients or customers
- open doors to speaking engagements or other opportunities for you
- add to your credibility
- elevate your status
- make you feel like even more of a winner

Let's get started.

Questions People Ask before They Write a Book

Can anyone write a book?

If certain things are true, anyone can write a book. Which things must be true?

- The person has or obtains experience or expertise in some topic.
- The person has or chooses the right mindset or determination.
- The person has a plan or recipe to follow.
- The person makes time to write the book.

Why write a book?

There are so many benefits to writing a book, both for you and your readers. Let's start with the generous goals first. My mentor, friend, and client Vincent Pugliese talks often about generosity. He taught about generous goals in his second book, *The Wealth of Connection*.

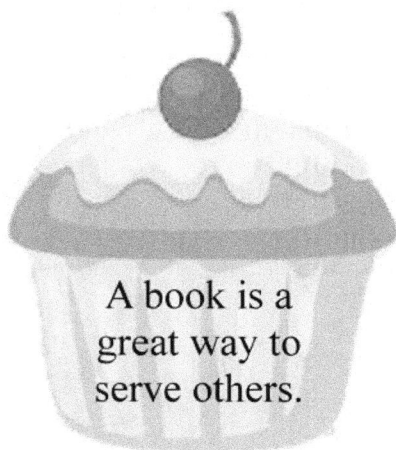

A book is a great way to serve others.

You have knowledge that other people need and experiences they can benefit from. Your goal is to serve them. If your book is a how-to, they'll have the opportunity to learn how to do whatever it is your book is about. If your book is inspirational, they could feel uplifted and then go do amazing things. No matter what type of book your nonfiction book is, it is going to benefit some readers.

They are waiting for your book, so give it to them. Before you can deliver it, you have to bake it. Before you can bake it, you need to have a good recipe to follow.

How does writing a book benefit me?

Being an author equates to being an authority. You'll notice that the word *authority* contains the word *author*. We've all heard it said, "She wrote the book on the subject." It isn't always literal, but it carries the message that writing a book means one is an expert on the topic.

Writing a book opens doors like nothing else can. It leads to opportunities to do more and to earn more. Kary Oberbrunner wrote *Your Book is Not a Business Card: How to turn your book into 18 streams of income*. Here are some of the income streams it mentions:

- Self-Study courses
- Live coaching
- Certifying coaches to teach your content
- Public speaking
- Content marketing
- Memberships and subscriptions
- High-End consulting
- Workshops
- Seminars and webinars
- Affiliate and referral partnerships

Even these things can be part of your generous goals. Imagine all the good you can do in the world with the power of a book.

A Baker's Dozen Reasons to Write a Book

1. You can serve people in many ways.
2. The research and writing processes give you great opportunities to build relationships.
3. Gathering market research can be part of the process.
4. You can show thought leadership and expertise.
5. Clients will be attracted to you if you do it right.
6. It's a good way to raise awareness for a cause or create a movement.
7. A book lends itself well to a signature talk, workshop, etc.
8. You can use it as a call to action (CTA) for your podcast, YouTube videos, TikTok videos, blog posts, and more.
9. Prospects appreciate it as a gift, and it can help you build relationship and authority with them.
10. You can create a legacy.
11. The expenses associated with researching, writing, editing, publishing, and marketing a book can be tax write-offs.
12. You can travel. Think about where you'd enjoy going, and then set up some book signings and a book thank-you tour like the ones Vincent Pugliese sets up after his books come out.
13. The personal growth you will experience as you go through the process is astounding.

But who am I to write a book?

You may be familiar with the term "impostor syndrome." It means that people who are high achievers feel less than worthy of their position. They feel as if they really aren't that good and that people might find out that they aren't so competent after all. Then the gingerbread house they've built will come crumbling down.

In reality, people do see others pretty accurately. If the person experiencing impostor syndrome were a fake, people would already know it. Those who experience impostor syndrome are great at what they do. Most are very competent and high achievers. It's just a matter of confidence. For whatever reason, we have a critical and limiting voice in our head. It tells us, "You aren't as skilled as you pretend to be, fraud." Remember this: that voice is wrong.

People who experience impostor syndrome stand in sharp contrast to the neighborhood narcissists.

Those cream horns think they know everything. They can do everything you can do but bigger, better, faster, more. In reality, they are puffed up and mostly air! They don't have much flavor to them, either. The blowhards are hilariously incompetent, and everyone else knows it.

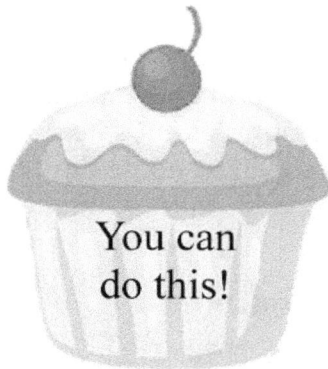

You can do this!

Almost everyone doubts themselves or their abilities from time to time. The only ones who don't are raging narcissists. If you sometimes wonder if you can or should do X, that's healthy. It's okay.

My impostor syndrome

In 1992, I started helping people become authors. Since then, I've had plenty of impostor syndrome moments. I've had the "Who am I to be doing this?" kinds of thoughts. In 2010, when I created the coaching program that led to my first book, I hadn't published any books. Some of my coaching clients had. I'd (ghost)written two, but the author never published them, so I wasn't sure how good my writing was. I didn't think the grades I received in college counted. (This is a perfect example of someone doubting and discounting their successes.)

I'm a firm believer in the practice of dragging things out into the light to get a better look at them. Many of our thoughts and beliefs exist because they're allowed to sit in a cool, dark place in the pantry of our heart. Once we pull them out and look at them, we can see that they're rotten and need replaced with something wholesome.

To address the thought of *"All I've written is . . ."* I pulled it out into the light to examine it. Here is how I did that.

I started to make a list of all the things I had written up to that point. This is what it looked like:

- a (book-length) manual for colleges seeking grants
- a few dozen grant proposals (some 100 pages long)
- a guide to the Southwest and Navajo culture
- more than 100 articles for online magazines
- about 200 radio commercials
- a survival guide for stay-at-home dads
- curriculum for schools and churches
- dozens of resumes and cover letters for clients
- some brochures, newsletters, sales letters, and business cards
- a guide to starting an in-home daycare
- hundreds of pages of online content

Disposing of sour flour

That's "all" I'd written by 2010. That's quite a bit. I'd written and edited too many academic and white papers to count. I'd also edited and proofread more than 50 books and manuals (more than 200 at the time of this writing). I had even coached some writers. Hey, I guess I was fairly qualified to coach writers after all. And that was 2010. I've been writing, editing, and coaching ever since.

Michael Hyatt is the former CEO of Thomas Nelson Publishers. He calls this level of expertise "The Sherpa." That is one who has been to the mountain and wants to help others do the same.

While writing that first book, whenever I had those impostor moments, I took a deep breath. I reminded myself of things I had done and what people had said about me and my abilities. Then I wrote a few more sentences. That's how I dealt with it.

That's how *you* will deal with it, too. Oh, yes, you'll have your own "impostor moments," times when you're not sure you can do the thing you want to do. I bet you have already had plenty of moments like that. If not, don't worry; they are coming. But now that you *know it* and exactly how to handle it, you'll learn how to ignore the doubt. Follow the recipe, and get back to writing.

These days, I rarely have impostor moments when I sit down to write a book or anything else. Note that I didn't say I never have them. I've been doing this for decades, and I still wonder from time to time if what I'm producing is any good. But determining whether it's good isn't up to me. It's up to the people who consume the content. It's my job to create it. That's your job, too.

How long does a book need to be?

There was a time when traditional publishing houses ran the writing world. Publishers believed that the heavier a book was, the more seriously the tome would be taken by buyers. They called it "the heft factor." Supposedly, the thicker the book, the more value it contained. We all know that's ridiculous. Most long books just repeat the same information over and over. They have more filler than flavor and more fluff than a cream puff. Better to deliver a small cake that has a great taste and will satisfy your reader.

How do I write a book?

You make a set of decisions and then follow a proven recipe. Tony Robbins says, "Success leaves clues." If you want to be successful at something, find someone who has done it, learn from them, and follow their path.

People have gone before you in authorship. Follow a path laid out by others. This book draws on the experience and expertise of people who followed a recipe before you. Because of that, it will help you. If you'd like to bake your book alongside others in Your Book Bakery and you're a good fit, then you're welcome to join us. More about that later. One step at a time.

Whisk Together

Make a list of things you have written before. Here are some things to include:

- letters
- emails
- stories
- blog posts
- reports
- lead magnets
- website content
- anything else you can think of

_____

_____

_____

_____

_____

_____

_____

_____

_____

_____

To decide whether you should write a book, answer the following questions.

Do you have some knowledge or expertise that others could use?

Does anyone pay money to find that knowledge or expertise in some way?

Is it important to make a difference in the world?

Are you willing to follow a proven path (recipe)?

If the answer to these questions is yes, then you should write a book.

Remember that time is short. In Orthodoxy, we say, "Memento mori." It means, "Remember that you will die" and serves as a reminder that we'd better make the most of our time on earth.

I know that's a heavy thought, and this book is about a lighthearted approach to writing. Why would I say that, then? Because it's a truth we all need to face. It will help us to get our books out of our heads and into the world, where they can do good things.

Make a list of all the things you might like to write someday — books, plays, songs, anything. Which of those will help others? Circle those. Which things could be part of your legacy? Put a star by those.

_____

_____

_____

_____

_____

_____

_____

_____

_____

_____

_____

_____

_____

_____

_____

_____

_____

_____

_____

_____

_____

Chapter 2: Now That You've Decided

Before you can write a book, you need to determine some things. Let's start with some questions about you and what you can bake up for the market.

Gold Zone Exercise

For many years, I've walked clients and students through what I call my Gold Zone Exercise. In recent years, I've seen several other authors and gurus doing a similar thing. Sometimes they put another circle or two in the Venn diagram.

This shows that many people can come up with the same idea when none of them knows that the others have come up with it. That's okay. It's good, even.

What if only one person thought of something and never took action on it?

The world would miss out on that tasty morsel. It's good for all of us that an idea often occurs to more than one person.

A large sheet of chart paper or a poster board is good for this activity. That size gives you plenty of room. If you don't have one of those, but you do have a white board or window available, use it. Grab some markers in different colors.

Draw three large, overlapping circles like this:

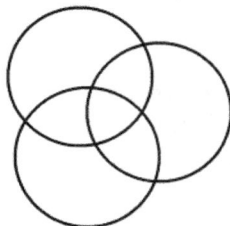

Make the upper left circle green (for money). Label it with something that indicates the circle will contain things people pay for. You might write "paying for" or put a dollar sign there: $. Then list everything you can think of that people are paying for. Not what you think they *would* pay for but what they *actually are* spending money on. Here are some examples:

births	clothing	writing implements
deaths	accessories	medications
waste removal	shelter	surgeries
food	travel	supplements
entertainment	music	sports
education	books	pampering

The next step in the exercise is to move to the upper right circle (make it red for "hot"). Jot down everything you can think of that you are good at doing or could quickly become good at doing.

The third step is to log things you'd be willing to do for 8–12 hours a day, at least until things really get cooking. Those things go in the lower left circle, which you'll make blue (for being loyal, sticking to it).

Writing in the overlapping portions comes next. Enter each of the items that are in both circle 1 and 2 into the overlapping area of those two circles. Do the same with the overlap of 2 and 3, and 1 and 3.

The final step is to put into the center only those things that are in all three circles. Most people end up with *one or two things*. That's their Gold Zone: the things they love, are excellent at, and could make a living doing.

In case you're concerned, one or two things in your Gold Zone will be enough.

Gold Zone for a Book

How does this exercise relate to writing a book? For the purposes of this book, you need to be skilled or knowledgeable in the area you want to write about. It needs to be something you enjoy well enough to stick with it through the tough times that are part of writing a book. It also needs to be about something that people are spending money on.

To apply the Gold Zone Exercise to writing your book, in circle #1, put things people are buying books about. To be clear, the book sales don't have to be numerous, but they do need to exist. If no one is buying *any* books on X, think long and hard about whether you want to take the time to write a book about X.

For the second circle, stick to the things you are already good at. You can redo the exercise later if you want to, when you have time to do more extensive research. For this book, you're going to write about something you already know a great deal about.

Take a look at your sheet. What do you have in your Gold Zone? Is it like one of these books about mindset and coaching?

- *Legendary* by my client Tommy Breedlove
- *Ungraduated* by my client Ken Hannaman

Is it a parenting guide for moms of multiples? Perhaps it's a book on bearded dragon care, like the one Heather Woosley wrote during a session of Your Book Bakery. Is it an inspirational book for people with disabilities?

Maybe it's one of these:

How-to guide to

- learning sign language
- exercising with arthritis
- homeschooling kids with ADHD
- caring for bearded dragons

Historic book about

- Depression-Era cooking
- American education
- parenting trends

Inspirational book about

- homeschooling
- overcoming adversity
- parenting a mentally ill child
- health and wellness

Informative book about

- the science of cooking
- Orthodox Christian doctrine
- health and wellness
- Navajo culture

Road map for

- homeschooling year round
- parenting solo
- strategic planning for a business

No matter which type of book you want to write, you'll need to make several decisions before you write the first word. And, as you can see, the same topic can be done in different ways. Take a look at the lists again, and you'll see homeschooling addressed four different ways.

The Foundational Questions

(AKA the not-so-dry ingredients)

Before you can start planning your book, you'll need to answer some questions. It's important to have the main ingredients on hand before you start creating something.

Sit with this part of the work for as long as you need to. If necessary, let it simmer in your brain for a few days, and then answer the questions. You'll need this information before you move forward. Substitutions are not permitted—not because I want to be mean but because they simply won't work.

On some of the questions, you're going to be guessing because you don't know the answers yet. All I ask is that you do the best you can. Make the guess. You might find out that your guess was wrong or things have changed. Simply adjust the answer to the question.

Some of the questions might seem irrelevant, but please stay with me. Their importance should become clear.

You don't need to try to squeeze in your answers or otherwise write anything on these two pages. The questions and statements will be repeated after some explanation. Then there will be plenty of space for you to write.

Questions about your audience

Who is my audience?

What do they need?

What do they want?

What keeps them up at night?

What are they buying to help them with their desire/need?

How can I serve them best with this book?

What is the path from A to B that I want to take my reader on?

Questions about your goals

What are my goals for this book?

Which items on this list are the most important?

What do I ultimately want to accomplish with it?

How do I want to grow through this process?

What would my life be like if I reach the goals related to my book?

Statements about your book

Describe in three sentences the book you want to write.

Describe your book in one sentence.

Who is my audience?

Imagine that you have various candies for topping desserts. Let's say there are peanut butter cups, gummy bears, suckers, fruit chews, and mints.

Each sweet represents the people in one of these categories:

- people who consume your content
- people who follow you on social media and other platforms
- people who listen to you
- people who learn from you
- people who ask for your advice

Here is another way to put this:

- your blog readers
- your podcast listeners
- your Facebook friends, TikTok and Instagram followers, and LinkedIn connections
- your students
- your friends and family

Just for fun, pick which candy represents which category of audience member to you. Draw a line connecting the pairs.

Now imagine scooping up all of the types of sugar bombs and putting them into a gallon-sized glass jar. That's your audience. Your audience comprises* the following:

- people who consume your content
- those who follow you on social media and other platforms
- people who listen to you
- the ones who learn from you
- individuals who ask for your advice

Write about your audience here.

_____

_____

_____

_____

_____

_____

Comprises means holds/contains. *Composed of* means to be made up of. *Consists of* means to be made up of. Almost every time you see or hear *comprises*, it is being used wrong.

What do they want?

The people you wish to serve, what do they want? If they want what you offer, fabulous. If they don't want it, though, or if they don't even know it exists or that it is for them, then you have a challenge. You might need to educate them over time. You also may have to sell them what they *want* and give them what they *need*.

Write about what your audience members want.

_____

_____

_____

_____

_____

What do they actually need?

As implied above, people often don't know what they need, and what they want and what they need are rarely the same thing. You have to know both if you're going to get in front of them and sell your book and other products and services to them most effectively.

Write here what you think they actually need.

_____

_____

_____

_____

_____

What keeps them up at night?

Every group worries about something or obsesses about something. New parents fret about feeding their baby and avoiding chemicals. Young people ruminate on their future careers and children of their own. Dog trainers and other service providers wonder how to get more clients. Are they doing everything they "should" to build their businesses?

Consider your audience—that jar full of gummy bears and mints. What do they wonder or worry about? It might disturb their sleep. What makes them keep opening the oven door to see if it's done baking yet?

Write out everything you can think of that keeps your audience members up at night.

_____

_____

_____

_____

_____

_____

_____

_____

_____

_____

The next question is, "What are they buying to help them with their desire/need?" I'll give you lines for writing the answer to this question right after the next segment. First, let's look at how to find out the answer to that question.

What are they buying?

How can you discover what people are buying? Amazon is the answer. Love it or lump it, we all have to admit that for now, at least, Amazon is the 800-pound gorilla cake. For the vast majority of us, it's the best place to put our books. It's also the best place to conduct market research when it comes to determining what people are buying.

Amazon.com is the largest bookseller in the world. Browse through their popular book listings. Look at completed sales on eBay as well to find out what people are buying.

Keyword research (KWR), which we'll look at in chapter 9, is also a good way to tell what people are looking for. That does not always translate to what they are willing to *pay* for. But there is a tool that can give you a solid idea of what books people are willing to pay for because they are doing it. That tool is Publisher Rocket, created by my Facebook friend Dave Chesson. Because it helps you with Amazon in general and not just KWR, I'll tell you about it here.

Publisher Rocket

Publisher Rocket is like the butane torch used to caramelize a crème brulé. Every Book Baker should have it. It's effective, affordable, and easy to use. I've used and recommended it for a long time because I love it. Just recently did I receive an affiliate link for it. That's the way it goes with anything I recommend. I only suggest things I do or would use myself. Your trust is something precious to me.

Publisher Rocket focuses exclusively on Amazon and gets all of its data from there. What works on Amazon may transfer to other marketplaces. Publisher Rocket helps you position your book effectively. To do that, you need to place your book in the right category and select the right keywords for it. Both can be hard. Fortunately, this tool makes it much easier.

Publisher Rocket also helps you analyze the competition:

- Discover which categories are saturated and which books are and are not selling.
- Analyze your competitors' earnings and book titles.
- Look at many books on one screen and see what is working in book covers.

You'll need to enter keywords when you upload your book. Using its Keyword Research feature, you can find the most profitable keywords in minutes.

Publisher Rocket can even help you determine how many books you need to sell to become a bestseller. It has many great features and can save you both time and money:

- real-time reporting (updated three times a day)
- resource library
- tutorials

It is well worth the price tag (around $100), and there's a 30-day money-back guarantee. I use this tool on my clients' books. I wouldn't be without it, and neither should you.

My affiliate link for Publisher Rocket is https://harshman6776--rocket.thrivecart.com/publisher-rocket/

Magazines as a sign

Counting the magazines available on a particular topic is a good way to determine if there's an audience for it. Magazines that don't sell well aren't published for long. If there are at least two magazines on your topic, it's selling.

Do a little quick research, and jot down notes here regarding what your audience members are buying to help them with their desire or need:

_____

_____

_____

_____

_____

_____

_____

_____

_____

Now add any thoughts you have on it. If you think they're being foolish or missing out by buying X, write that down. In the next segment, we'll talk about how you can provide something better for them so they won't have to do that anymore.

_____

_____

_____

_____

_____

_____

_____

_____

How can I serve them best with this book?

You've answered questions about who your audience is, what they want and need, and what keeps them up at night. Now think about how you can best serve them with the book you're going to write.

There is no one right answer here. These are not exclusionary. If you choose one, it does not mean you cannot also choose another. You might find that more than one fits your situation.

Should you select one small problem and give them a bite-sized solution to it?

Should you spread out a path for a larger issue?

Would it be best to inform them about a situation and options?

Would a cookbook feed them best?

Using the Venn diagram technique, you could find an ideal book for you to write. Find the intersection of three of their needs or characteristics. In this case, a cookbook of keto desserts would be a great fit!

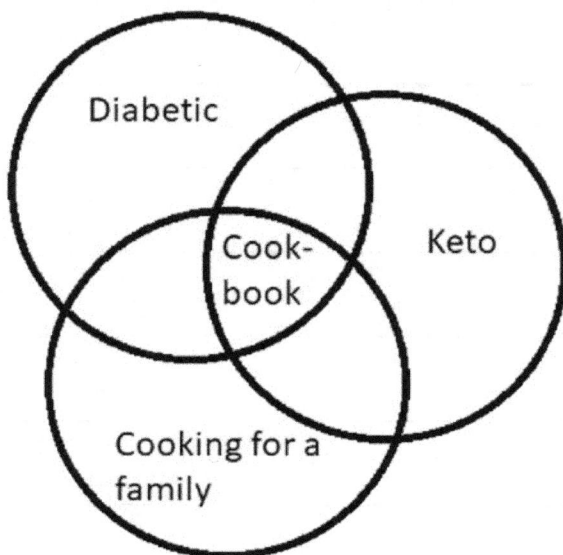

What is the path from A to B that I want to take my reader on?

A nonfiction book author worth their salt helps to create transformation. This occurs in the reader or in the reader's life. The book needs to take the reader from Point A to Point B.

Where are they before they pick up your book? (This probably is not a literal location but more likely an emotional state or a life situation.) Are they unemployed, homeless, or struggling with their job and bills? Perhaps they feel depressed and disbelieve that their life can get better. Or they could be doing well and desiring more.

Where do you want to take them by the time they're finished reading your book?

Maybe you want them to have a job they enjoy. Dan Miller wanted that for the readers of his book *48 Days to the Work and Life You Love.*

You could want them to change their beliefs, take action, and get some results. Susie Tomenchok wanted that for her readers. She wrote *The Art of Everyday Negotiation without Manipulation.*

Perhaps like Mary Valloni did with her book, *Fundraising Freedom: 7 Steps to Build and Sustain Your Next Campaign*, you want your readers to be well-equipped for a particular task or role. (Yes, it was tempting to put "roll" there, but I just could not bring myself to do it. I am an editor, after all).

How do I determine that path?

Finding a niche

Aspiring business people, including writers, frequently hear, "Find your niche." This refers to a small and very focused segment of the market. Bass Pro doesn't try to reach every sportsman. They don't even aim at all fishermen (a smaller segment of the sporting market). They sell products aimed at *only bass fishermen*. Premier Angler niches down even more. They sell products for bass fishermen who are also disabled.

What does that have to do with writing and publishing your book, you ask? Authors and other writers also need to find their niche. That's the area where their writing fits best, their audience. Debby Mayne's niche is Christian women's fiction. Adrienne Z. Milligan's niche is gluten-free living due to celiac disease. Dan Miller's niche is career. If you already have an audience, great! You are ahead. You'll want to create your book with them in mind. Answer the following questions anyway.

Making a decision

Choose an audience you want to serve and a problem you want to help them solve. One great approach is to write what's obvious to you but complicated or invisible to others.

If something is easy for you, and you can't imagine why it's hard for other people, that's a skill/gift/talent/genius you have. Make use of it.

We all have knowledge and perspectives that others do not. Sharing those things is what writing is for. If it's something your audience needs and will pay for, it might be the perfect topic for your book.

Who is your ideal audience? You might choose to serve your current or future clients. Write about them in detail.

_____

_____

_____

_____

_____

_____

_____

What are their biggest challenges?

_____

_____

_____

_____

_____

_____

What keeps them up at night?

_____

_____

_____

_____

_____

What do they need?

_____

_____

_____

_____

_____

What do they want?

_____

_____

_____

_____

_____

Which of those do you want to help them with?

_____

_____

How can you best serve them with your book?

_____

_____

_____

_____

What do you want your book to be about?

_____

_____

_____

_____

You want to take your reader from Point A to Point B. What are those points?

_____

_____

_____

_____

What is the general path? We'll gather more information during the research and outlining phase. For now, just jot down the general path from Point A to Point B.

_____

_____

_____

_____

Where do they spend their time?

_____

_____

_____

_____

What are three to five products or services your readers want that you don't yet offer?

_____

_____

_____

_____

How could you offer those products/services?

_____

_____

_____

_____

What are my goals for this book?

Define your goals. Asking yourself the following questions will help:

What matters most from the list below? Least? Number them from 1 to 10. Feel free to add your own as well, and be sure to number them, too.

_____ Earning money directly from book sales

_____ Opening doors for speaking engagements, trainings, or similar opportunities

_____ Obtaining media interviews and leverage them to promote your business

_____ Serving readers with the material between the covers of the book

_____ Attracting clients

_____ Showing family/friends what can be accomplished

_____ Building new revenue streams around your book

_____ Increasing self-confidence by completing this project

_____ Building an audience for future books

_____ Getting paid to write for magazines and other outlets

Here is one author's list.

What matters most from the list below? Least? Number them from 1 to 10.

1. *Serving readers* with the material between the covers of the book
2. *Opening doors* for speaking engagements, trainings, or similar opportunities
3. *Earning money* directly from book sales (for charity work)
4. *Showing family/friends* what can be accomplished
5. *Increasing self-confidence* by completing this project
6. *Building an audience* for future books
7. Obtaining media interviews and leverage them to promote your business
8. Getting paid to write for magazines and other outlets
9. Building new revenue streams around your book
10. Attracting clients

What do I ultimately want to accomplish with this book?

_____

_____

_____

_____

_____

What opportunities can I create with this book?

_____

_____

_____

_____

How do I want to grow through this process?

_____

_____

_____

_____

What would my life be like if I reach the goals related to my book?

_____

_____

_____

_____

_____

Statements about your book

Describe in three sentences the book you want to write.

_____

_____

_____

_____

_____

_____

_____

One of my students, author Perry Gabbard, shared this draft slide on one of the video calls for the program Your Book Bakery:

Book summary: What is the book about? *Adventure & Transformation*

- **Three sentence:** A seeker sets off on a quest to backpack from Mexico to Canada on the Pacific Crest Trail. Along the way he experiences challenges, high adventure, indescribable beauty, and a deeply intimate walk with God. As you follow along, you will *find a way forward:* 1) Renewing your lost or forgotten dreams, 2) Deepening your connection with God, and 3) Finding clear direction to begin your own unique journey.

- **Book type:** A "Bit-N-Piece Book"
  - Titled: "To Return, Retreat, and Renew. A 40 day journey of adventure & transformation."
  - A book that you can slip into and out of easily.
  - Easy to read a chapter a day, think about it, and use the accompanying journal to discover your own vision and way forward

- **40 short chapters:** 40 days of reading with ~600-700 words per chapter
  - Snapshots in time along Perry's Pacific Crest Trail Adventure
  - Short and sweet. 3-4 pages of writing with 50 word ending for "personal application" (so what about you?)
  - *Easy to read, but personally challenging*

- **4 sections:**
  - Introduction – The call of wilderness and the restoration of a unfulfilled dream
  1. Fall – A season to Return
  2. Winter – A season of Retreat
  3. Springtime– A season to Renew
  4. Summer - A season to Recapture

Describe your book in one sentence. Here's an example that would work for Perry's book.

Getting outdoors can help people connect with God, however they know him to be.

Thesis statement

Soon, you will make an assertion or statement that your book will make (even if subconsciously) to a reader. You may use your one-sentence description, but you don't have to. First, I want to show you some examples so it will be easier for you to write the thesis statement for your book.

Here's one. Fully engaged people are happy to help you spread the word about your business, product, or service. The book I'm thinking of that this statement fits is *This Is Marketing* by Seth Godin.

Here are some more examples. See if you can match the statement with the book's title. Draw a line from a statement to the title you think it fits. You won't have to wait long to see how many you got right. The answers are at the bottom of the page in the form of the authors' names. One has been done for you.

Statement

1. Networking doesn't have to be slimy.

2. Reach out and be generous and helpful, and you'll have all the success you want.

3. You have creative potential and can unlock it.

4. Anyone can write a book if they have all of the ingredients and a recipe to follow.

5. Answer the questions your customers ask, and you'll position yourself as *the* resource.

6. You can have your dream work and life within 48 days.

7. No one is born a legend, but anyone can become one.

8. Negotiating can be fun!

9. The right question helps you practice accountability and make better choices in the moment.

10. You can make money several ways at once.

Book

48 Days to the Work and Life You Love by Dan Miller

Your Book Bakery: Making it easy to write a book by Jennifer Harshman

Legendary by Tommy Breedlove

QBQ: The Question Behind the Question by John G. Miller

The Referral of a Lifetime by Tim Templeton

Multiple Streams of Income by Ryan Reger

The Wealth of Connection by Vincent Pugliese

They Ask, You Answer by Marcus Sheridan

The Artist's Suitcase: 26 Essentials for the creative journey by Kent Sanders

The Art of Everyday Negotiation without Manipulation by Susie Tomenchok

1. Tim Templeton 2. Vincent Pugliese 3. Kent Sanders 4. Jennifer Harshman 5. Marcus Sheridan 6. Dan Miller 7. Tommy Breedlove 8. Susie Tomenchok 9. John G. Miller 10. Ryan Reger

Statement	Book
11. Not all of the stereotypes about this generation are true, and here's how to work with them.	*Beyond Normal: A field guide to embrace adventure, explore the wilderness, and design an extraordinary life with kids* by Heidi Dusek
12. Having these lizards as pets is easier than you think.	*$1,000 100 Ways* by Nick Loper
13. Managing your writing like a project makes you more effective.	*Jį Dóó Tłee, Day and Night* by Nedra Emery
14. These real people made money on the side, and you can, too.	*Bearded Dragons: The care and feeding of tiny dinosaurs* by Heather Hollingsworth Woosley
15. Conflict can be resolved and even prevented.	*The Millennial Whisperer* by Chris Tuff
16. Building habits can be easy.	*Ungraduated: Finding your why and dropping out of outdated belief systems* by Ken Hannaman
17. You get to choose the kind of person you'll be.	The PLAY NICE in Your Sandbox series by Ron Price
18. Having kids doesn't have to mean a boring life.	*Project Management for Writers* by Terry Stafford
19. This bilingual book is the Navajo myth of how the 24-hour time cycle came to be divided into light and darkness	*Personality Isn't Permanent* by Dr. Benjamin Hardy
20. You can leave systems that don't serve you.	*Atomic Habits* by James Clear

11. Chris Tuff 12. Heather Hollingsworth Woosley 13. Terry Stafford, PMP 14. Nick Loper 15. Ron Price 16. James Clear 17. Dr. Benjamin Hardy 18. Heidi Dusek 19. Nedra Emery 20. Ken Hannaman

Whisk Together

It's important to be able to say what your book is about, who it's for, and so on. Many people will ask you, but it's not just for them. It's for you! When you know what you're doing, for whom, and why, staying focused and motivated is so much easier. The sentence you're about to write can also help with your cover design and text on your cover.

Fill in the blanks.

My book helps _____,

who struggle with _____,

to do _____

so that they can _____.

Note that the commas might not be needed in your actual sentence. Here are some examples.

My book helps business owners who struggle with getting enough clients to know what to blog about, so that they can establish themselves as the expert and grow their business. (*They Ask You Answer* by Marcus Sheridan)

My book helps stressed-out business owners who struggle with saying no and taking care of themselves to prioritize their mental health so that they can feel relief while still being productive. (A forthcoming, as yet untitled book by M.J. James)

My book helps writers who struggle with being productive enough to build a daily writing habit so that they can meet their goals, whether it's to finish a book or make a living as a writer. (*The Daily Writer* by Kent Sanders)

Write a possible thesis statement for your book here.

_____

_____

Chapter 3: Overview of the Entire Process

Most of the complicated undertakings in our world have a process that can be followed. This is true of writing a book. Here, you'll find an overview of the entire process. Later, you'll begin following the recipe to create your book.

The Stages

The Prewriting Stage
(Shopping for Ingredients)

Researching

This includes the research you'll need for outlining, writing, and positioning. It could include determining whom you'll ask to endorse your book and which podcasts you want to go on to promote it.

Outlining and other planning (book structure, chapter structure)

After you've conducted the research needed for outlining your book, you'll need to outline your book.

The Writing Stage
(Setting up Your Kitchen)

Once your outline is created, if you've done it well, then it's just a matter of filling in the blanks. You're free to write the sections of your book in any order you choose. Often, smart cookies skip around in their outline. This is the longest phase for authors who are writing books about things they know deeply. For other authors, researching can be the longest phase.

Write a bad first draft as fast as you can. Of course, you will go back to it later and clean it up. These are the only goals for the first draft:

- Follow a good outline.
- Get it done.

The outline is to make sure your book is organized. Why a speed requirement? One of the biggest obstacles between desiring and doing is overcoming self-doubt. The way to get momentum is to start moving. The way to make progress is to keep moving.

The Post-Writing Stage (Shaping the Cake)

There are several steps involved in producing a book after it's been drafted. Each phase of the process involves different actions and takes time. Here is some information about each one we take authors through and what it looks like. I want to give you an overview before you begin working on your book.

Editing

This stage doesn't take much of the author's time personally (hands-on). It does take calendar time, so you should allow for that.

When it comes to editing, there are several steps. Please note that this is the only industry I'm aware of that does not have standardized terms for things. Terminology in the medical field is clear. If a surgeon were to walk into an operating room, hold out one hand, and say, "Scalpel," no one would deliver a rib spreader. Some use these terms to mean something other than what we mean:

- developmental editing
- line editing
- copy editing
- proofreading

Be sure to ask what they mean when they say X. For solid definitions of editing terminology, see *Find a REAL Editor: Avoiding the posers and scammers*. The e-book is free on Amazon. It's available in paperback as well.

Most editors require at least 50% up-front payment. Final payment is made before the final files and copyright are released back to the client. This is an industry-standard practice implemented to prevent theft of services. Once payment is complete, the files and rights are released to the author.

Because there are different types of editing, and each one takes time, allow plenty of time for this stage. One of the biggest mistakes new authors make is setting a launch date for their book before it's edited. The first step in editing is manuscript evaluation.

Manuscript evaluation

Our evaluator reads through manuscripts and assesses them. Then we offer the appropriate package, if any. We only work with certain types of books. If something is not a good fit for us, we are usually happy to refer the author to someone else.

My number-one goal is to get you what you need, even if we're not it. That is a core value of my company.

An evaluation includes attention to the following:

- overall structure and organization
- strength of ideas
- punctuation
- grammar
- spelling
- syntax
- style
- flow

This process includes looking at the structure as well as the contents.

A note for the worried author: We work using Tracked Changes. When you get your manuscript back, you can go over any stylistic changes and decide whether to accept them. Our subjective changes are opinions based on our experience and expertise. We present the suggestion. You decide. It's your book and your call.

Even if they don't say it, many authors fear that an editor will steal their book and make it their own. That's rare. It never happens at Harshman Services.

We make suggestions. We tell you how the dictionary spells it and what the rules are.

Then you make your choices because you have to live with your book. No one should have control over it except for you.

Not sure what you need? That's extremely common, and it's okay. We evaluate every manuscript that comes through our virtual doors. We can help you know what your manuscript needs. We also do a free sample copy edit to show you what our work looks like on your writing.

Who can't bake with us

After an evaluation, if you or we don't feel like it's a good fit, that's okay. We may recommend some colleagues outside our company.

Please know that we will not help people who write harmful things. That means we don't serve everyone. It also means we don't always make referrals.

One example of this is a male author who had never been married but wrote a book telling women that they should carry the entire weight of the household, marriage, and children—and submit to abusive husbands.

I checked to be sure I had not time-traveled to the Dark Ages. This was not long before the year 2020.

No. Nope. Huh-uh, buddy. Not on my watch. We were not about to help someone brainwash women into tolerating abuse and believing it was "God's will for their lives."

He then had the gall to ask, "But could you refer me to someone else?"

My thought was, *No way. I wouldn't wish that on any editor or reader on this planet.* My words were polite, though. I said I could not.

Surprise, surprise: he then became abusive to me and derided me for being a woman.

You're going to write good and helpful things, though, so there shouldn't be anything to worry about there.

Developmental editing phase

Be prepared for some big changes. The manuscript you worked so long and hard to write may need major surgery. Entire sections may be removed. Chapters might be moved around, shortened, lengthened, or combined. You might receive suggestions to add anecdotes or to feature other people in your book. This does not detract from your expertise, as many authors think it will. It strengthens it.

Here's what we do in this phase.

Developmental editing is a "big-picture" type of edit. The goal is to examine both the content and organization of your manuscript. Your editor will make suggestions regarding these elements and more:

- content
- organization
- appropriateness
- order of the chapters
- chapter structure
- the reader's journey
- the book's purpose
- applicability to your audience

Your editor will also rearrange sections if necessary. They will suggest headings and chapter titles if needed. This makes them more memorable or effective.

In this phase, we will also conduct a plagiarism check. This is not because we suspect any kind of wrongdoing on your part. It can be difficult to remember where all you have heard/read things, and it is important to cite all of your sources. To help you with this, we run each manuscript through Copyscape or a similar tool.

A developmental editor never works on spelling, grammar, or typos. That requires a different type of thinking. Very few people can do both developmental editing *and* mechanical editing. Mechanical includes copy editing. Copy editing is work that a different type of editor does, and it comes later in the process. The developmental editor focuses on the flow of the manuscript from start to finish. Ignore any mistakes you see when the manuscript comes back to you after developmental editing.

Here's how long it usually takes: Each round usually takes one week per 10,000 words. The author is welcome to take longer when the book is with them. Usually, we do two rounds, and it looks like this: editors, client, editors, client. But we will do as many rounds as necessary. This is the longest and hardest phase.

Self-care is important. You may feel like you've been told to go back to the drawing board. Some authors have entered major depressive episodes upon receiving their developmental edits.

We are gentle. We treat our clients with respect. The way we treat you makes it much easier, but it's still a challenge for most authors. That's normal.

When you get your book back, please take extra good care of yourself. Take your time working through the edits and revisions. Read through the entire thing first without making any changes. Give it a day or two to rest in your brain. Then process no more than 10,000 words a day, taking breaks and resting more than you think you need to.

Line editing phase

Here's what we do in this phase. In line editing, we examine each sentence for best wording and clarity. We determine if the material is appropriate for the intended audience. Is there too much terminology? We make sure the reading level is correct and not too high or low. Then we examine each sentence for wording, clarity, and fit. Does the sentence fit in the paragraph? Does the paragraph fit in the section? We look at your book line by line.

We want to be sure the languaging is appropriate. This is the type of editing that is often needed by new authors or those with challenges such as dyslexia. It's also needed for authors who use terminology their readers might not know.

In a line edit, your editor will polish and reword sentences to improve clarity and flow. They will also reduce repetition, wordiness, awkwardness, and overuse of passive voice.

A line edit includes addressing poor sentence structure. It also reduces what is called "purple prose" (overly ornate writing).

When my manuscript went through line editing, the number of "very hard to read" sentences went from 38 out of 3,850 to 2.

Do not expect a line editor to make corrections to your spelling, grammar, and punctuation. Look instead for comments like the following:

- The Flesch reading level of this book is grade level 8.2. For general audiences, no higher than grade 6 is recommended. (The book you're reading right now is at level 4).
- Change at least 50% of the contractions to the full two words (*don't* becomes *do not*).
- Use words that have fewer syllables.
- This section has some wordy sentences. Delete any words that are not needed.
- Keep each sentence to only one idea. Break complicated sentences into two or three.
- Simplify the structure of the sentences. Eliminate or at least reduce the number of compound-complex sentences.
- Make these paragraphs shorter. Remember this saying and acronym: Intersections can take us in new directions and are made of STREETS. Start a new paragraph when any of the following is true.
  - The **S**peaker changes.
  - **T**ime passes.
  - The **R**eader needs a break from a long paragraph.
  - **E**mphasis or **E**motion shifts.
  - The **T**opic/**T**one changes.
  - A new **S**cene begins.
- Use more headings, subheadings, bulleted lists, graphics, charts, and infographics.

Here's how long it usually takes: This phase usually takes two to four weeks. Most of the changes in a line edit are subjective, a matter of opinion. You get to consider them and decide which ones to keep and which ones to reject. Changes to readability should usually be accepted.

Copy editing phase

It is important for you to know that most of the changes made in this phase are mandatory. Those that are optional will have comments connected with them. We use Track Changes to be transparent and show you what we've done, not to say that the changes are optional. This not only is honest on our part, but it also helps authors see how much work we do on their manuscripts. If the author chose a package without dev. ed., then the plagiarism check will be done here.

Here's how long it usually takes: two to four weeks.

To ensure the highest quality work, we limit our editors to processing 10,000 words per day. This reduces error fatigue. Your editor will do the following:

- standardize notes, bibliographies, and reference lists
- make style decisions based on the Chicago Manual of Style
- source citations
- determine whether to spell out numbers or leave them as numerals
- determine whether to italicize or use quotation marks
- check that military titles, job positions, and business department names are treated correctly

Your copy editor will also correct problems with these:

- grammar
- spelling
- punctuation
- capitalization
- syntax

- word usage
- pronouns (him/her, who/whom, etc.);
- foreign words
- quotations

In other words, in this type of edit, your editor will look after the myriad details. The changes to spelling, grammar, and punctuation are different from developmental edits. These changes are mandatory. Some authors think they know better than their editor, so they reject those changes. That leaves their book full of errors. Then they get bad reviews for poor editing. That makes the editor look inept when in fact, the author is the one at fault. Please be smart about this. Accept all changes, or go with the "clean version" we send you after the copy editing has been done.

Fact checking phase (optional)

In this phase, our fact checker goes through a manuscript. Names, dates, locations, events, statistics, data, and anything else pertinent is checked. We make sure it is all correct. If anything is not, we fix it and cite a source.

It would be a shame to invest all the time, effort, and money into a book only to be discredited by a few factual errors. This process takes about two weeks for most books. If the book is heavy on the facts, it will definitely take longer.

Here's how long it usually takes: month should be allocated for this phase if it's chosen.

Design/Layout/Formatting phase

Formatting is the process of making a book look like a book. First, we turn a Microsoft Word document into an InDesign file. Then we turn the ID file into a PDF and e-pub that are ready for publishing.

Here's how long it usually takes: about a month. The interior designer needs all photos and other images at the right size and resolution.

Book Cover

We address the book cover here because it is part of the design phase. But the cover cannot be finalized until after all editing and layout are complete. The exact page count is needed to determine the size of the cover.

This is an area where very few authors should even consider a DIY approach. You might end up with a cover that looks like one of these DIY covers:

Smart authors want to avoid looking bad. Some claim they don't let the cover influence their decision to buy a book. We think they say that because they don't want to appear to be judgmental.

A book's cover influences nearly everyone's decision on whether or not to buy that book.

You want your book cover to look professional, like one of these:

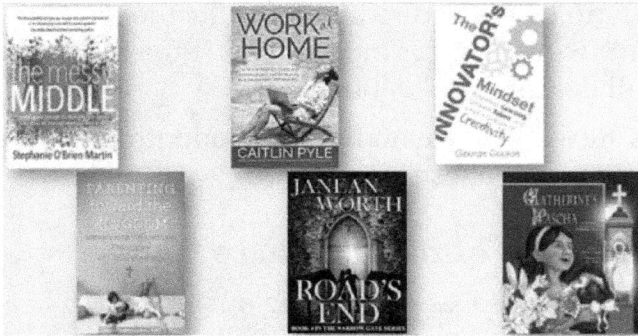

We have created an intake form that designers love. One told me she had never thought of asking all the questions up front. She always ended up doing several rounds of back-and-forth, wasting so much time. I'd rather help the designer gather the ingredients and know the recipe up front. That beats trying to guess what the author wants the frosting to look and taste like. This applies to both the interior design/layout and the book cover.

We have our clients fill out that cover design intake form. That's where you put all your ideas, examples of covers, images, fonts, and colors you like. Do it as early as possible. You'll work with your designer to create an appropriate cover for your book.

Please know that you might have an idea (for your cover) that just won't work well. There are certain elements and conventions of design that you might not be familiar with. Hold loosely your likes and dislikes. Trust the designer to know what makes a good cover and what does not. Also, your cover designer should know all of the specifications for your book.

Beware purchasing premade covers or of working with someone who claims to be able to do your cover at any time. If the spine dimensions are incorrect, the printer (often Amazon) will reject the file. Readers who want your book won't be able to buy it. There is a wide range of pricing when it comes to covers as well as a wide range of talent/skill when it comes to designers.

One good way to approach this is to look at covers you like and find out who the cover designer was. You may need to ask the publisher. The cover designer may not be credited on the copyright page. Then contact that person and ask about working together on your cover. Be prepared for a price ranging up to $2,000 for a professionally designed cover.

Here's how long it usually takes: one to four weeks.

Proofreading phase

Here's what we do in this phase. This is a true proofread. Most of the time when you hear someone use the word *proofread*, they are using it wrong. They are talking about a copy edit. A proofread is an examination of the proof: the laid-out and printed book. After the book has been laid out, we go over it with a fine-toothed comb. We examine every character, heading, image, and anything else you can think of.

Here is how long it usually takes: one week.

This is a final check of your document before it's published. We look for minor mistakes in punctuation, spacing, and so on. Editors have been through the file. It has been laid out and formatted, and this is normally the last look to try to catch things that were missed. Every book has some mistakes. We just try to make sure that ours have as few as possible.

Test reads

We offer something no one else does: test reading. When everyone who has worked on the book thinks it is ready to go to press, rather than hitting Publish, we hit Pause. Then we send it to two or three team members who have never seen the manuscript. They go over it and look for any remaining errors.

To be clear, no book is going to be perfect. Some errors will remain no matter how much work is put into a book. Reasonable expectations are required. That said, we do our best to approach perfection. We give it that extra polish no one else does. Think of it as glitter on the frosting, if you'd like.

Here's how long it usually takes: Allow one week. In the next segment, we'll talk about publishing.

Publishing
(Putting Your Cake in the Display)

Publishing is the process of putting a book (or other work) out into the world for others to see it. Most people think it's everything that happens after the draft is written. Those are actually steps that lead up to publishing.

Where to publish your book

"How do I get published?" or "Where should I publish my book?" are questions nearly every one of my clients has asked me. To be able to answer that question, I need to know the topic of the book. If it doesn't have mass appeal, traditional publishing is out. I also need to know about the author's current platform. If it isn't at least 50,000 audience members strong, traditional publishing is out.

Fortunately, there are options for publishing today that weren't viable 30 years ago. These are storefronts available to authors now:

- traditional publishing houses
- self-publishing
- assisted self-publishing
- hybrid houses

The first and the last in this list are bad ideas for 95% of authors today. Two reasons were given above as to why traditional publishing isn't the avenue to pursue. Most "hybrid houses" are dirt cakes covered in pretty frosting. Beware.

Self-publishing, alone or assisted, is the way to go for almost everyone these days.

What is self-publishing?

Self-publishing is publishing your book yourself. Ideally, it looks like this:

- You write the book.
- You have it edited by an independent editing professional (like me).
- You have it formatted correctly for printing.
- Have it proofread by one professional, then have a final proof done by another.

- You get an ISBN for your book.
- You have a cover designer create a cover for the book.
- You have it printed by a printer who specializes in books.
- You'll need to place it with a book distributor to get it into bookstores, or just put it on Amazon and other platforms.

If you do all these things, you will have a book that is much easier to sell than Mr. Van Ity's book is.

You can sell your book through your website or blog. Your book can be on Amazon and in other online and physical locations, too. Your local bank and library may allow you to place a stack of your books there for sale because you're a local author. I've even seen books about the region for sale in pharmacies! That's not the typical place I'd expect to buy a book on hiking and local parks. But hey, if it works… And I know where to take *my* books when it's time to sell them, too!

Amazon and Draft2Digital are quite beneficial for most authors. Over the years, they have improved their systems, streamlining the process for authors. Amazon has even added hardback covers now.

Amazon

Here's what we do in this phase. Due to Amazon's rules, the author has to create their own account and upload their own book. We've taken authors through the process many times. Amazon does lay it out step by step for you, and it is time-consuming. It's easier for someone who has done it repeatedly.

The author gets on a Zoom call with one of us, and we walk the author through the process of uploading the book to Amazon. We provide keywords, help the author write the book description, and so forth.

It takes some time for Amazon to approve the book, from a matter of hours to a week or more.

The author then orders proof copies from Amazon and has a few trusted friends look for typos. Then the author reports them to us. We also look for any remaining errors. Then our typesetter makes the changes.

Here's how long it usually takes: about two weeks. Then the author announces to the world that the book is published.

Draft2Digital

Here's what we do in this phase. As soon as the book is ready on Amazon, we publish it to Draft2Digital. This makes the electronic version of the book (e-book) available at Barnes and Noble, Kobo, etc.

Here's how long it usually takes: one to two days.

The author then announces to the world that the book is available in those locations.

Editing other pieces

At Harshman Services, we edit anything connected to your book free of charge:

- blog posts
- press releases
- other materials

We are dedicated to helping your book succeed. Other editors and agencies do not offer that, to my knowledge, so be prepared to pay for it. I do recommend having someone edit everything that is connected to your book, so that you can look your best.

We offer ongoing blog content management packages for a fee. See the resources section for what the different packages contain.

For Smart Cookies

A one-stop shop is a smart choice because it saves you time and money. My guess is that you're not made of money, and you're probably not a project manager. Wasting your time is a choice you *could* make, but it's probably not one you *would* make.

You could find several service providers and spend the cash and the time needed to manage all of them. Or you could go with a one-stop shop, which is an agency that provides everything you need. Here's a short video that explains more about the benefits of a one-stop shop: https://www.youtube.com/watch?v=hpdkSJGVqnc

Whisk Together

Note what you've learned so far.

_____

_____

_____

_____

_____

_____

_____

_____

_____

_____

_____

_____

Make a list of questions you have at this point.

_____

_____

_____

_____

_____

_____

_____

_____

_____

_____

_____

_____

_____

Write what you hope to learn by the end of this book.

_____

_____

_____

_____

_____

_____

_____

_____

_____

_____

_____

_____

_____

Part Two
Gathering the Ingredients:
Tools and information you need
to write a book

In this section, we talk about tools and information you need to write a book.

You need to know a few things:

- what is involved in writing a book
- whom to ask for help
- which resources are available
- how much pricing may be
- what protocol is
- and so on

You'll also need a little data that will go into your book. You'll gather that in the research phase.

Here's something crucial you need to be doing every day for the rest of your life: connecting with other people.

When you work out your schedule, set some time for contacting people daily. You'll be sending a tiny treat to at least 3 per day for the next 90 days. It will benefit you to do at least that many every day, forever. The "treat" can be a message, a card, or anything else you'd like. It doesn't have to take up a lot of space, time, or money.

Why should you do this? To build your relationships. First of all, do it because it's the right thing to do. Another reason is the day will come when you want something, such as an endorsement or purchase of your book. If you wait to connect with people until you need something, you'll come across as a jerk. That approach is selfish. Most people will be offended by it. Do networking the right way.

To learn about networking the right way, read *The Referral of a Lifetime* by Tim Templeton. Then read *The Wealth of Connection* by Vincent Pugliese. Now, let's take a look at tools and other information you'll need.

Chapter 4: Setting up Your Kitchen

Commit. Clear the decks. Construct your book-baking space. Then use it.

Commit to doing this. We'll get to the "hows" part of it. First come the "whys" and the "whats."

By the end of Chapter 2, you knew why you want to write a book. Chapter 3 gave you an overview of the entire process, so now you know a lot of the "whats" that are involved. This chapter helps you set up your kitchen, putting into place those "whats" so that we can get to more of the "hows."

Discipline

As Jocko Willink said, discipline is freedom. Paradoxically, there is freedom within constraints.

For some people, the word *discipline* has negative connotations.

Joanna Penn says, "You don't need discipline if you have a why because you have a positive reason that drives you to the page. You want to be there."

Unfortunately, that's not always the case, especially with nonfiction writing. We have to show up and do the work, and often, we don't feel like it.

Seth Godin told me something on a Zoom call in January 2019. We professionals have to show up and do the work whether we feel like it or not. If someone does not have to show up and do the work, then they are not a professional but a fortunate amateur.

Have you ever seen a quotation attributed to more than one person? For this one, it's William Faulkner and Somerset Maugham.

"I only write when inspiration strikes. Fortunately, it strikes at nine every morning."

Regardless of who said it, it holds truth. This quotation is talking about what I call the ABCs of writing: Apply Butt to Chair.

Steven Pressfield wrote about The Resistance. That's the difficulty we all face when it comes to creating. Resistance is relentless. It comes in several shapes and flavors (some of them are even tasty). One is impostor syndrome. To overcome resistance, it's important to be aware and keep mixing your batter. It may never go away, but you can still produce delicious things in spite of it.

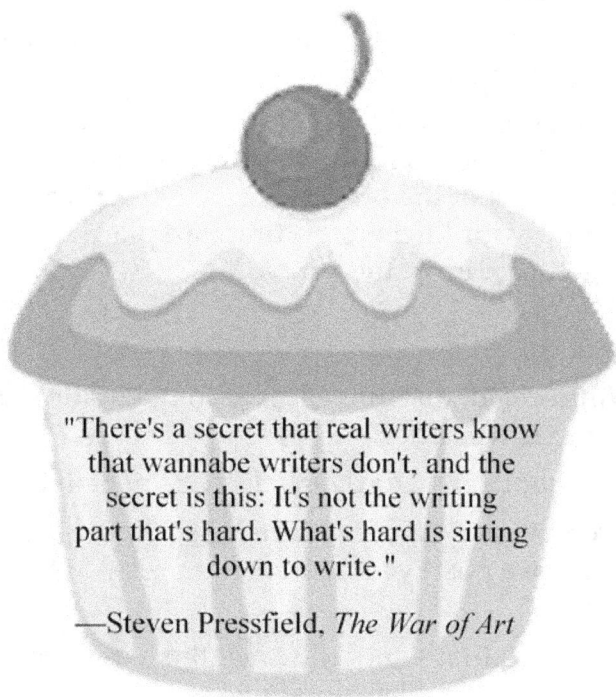

"There's a secret that real writers know that wannabe writers don't, and the secret is this: It's not the writing part that's hard. What's hard is sitting down to write."

—Steven Pressfield, *The War of Art*

Productivity Principles

Being productive, getting the book written, is one of the hardest things for an author to do. A factor in that is time—having insufficient room in the schedule for it. Bigger factors are fear and lacking a system, a framework. If you have the right things in place and you use your systems and follow your recipe, you will produce a book.

Let's look at some of the principles that will help you be productive and get your book written.

Pareto's Principle

Pareto's Principle is also called the 80/20 Rule. It states that approximately 80% of the results come from approximately 20% of the causes. In an organization, 20% of the people are doing 80% of the work. The other 80% of the people together are doing the remaining 20% of the work. It can also show up in even greater differences—95% of the work is being done by 5% of the people. You know this principle to be true, even if you were never able to express it this way. Just think about the workplaces, organizations, or churches you have been part of. A handful was doing almost all of the work!

In baking, a small number of the ingredients constitute the majority of the weight. The remaining ingredients only take up a small percentage of it. Just check any food label to see this in real life. It says something like, "Contains 2% or less of each of these items on this ginormous list of ingredients."

Of 100 tasks, 20 of them provide 80% (or more) of the results. The other 80 items (if you do them) provide the remaining 20% of the results. Here's the goal.

1. Determine which 20 items will give you 80% of the results.
2. Do them.
3. Put very little emphasis on the other 80 items.

For example, let's list ten chores in a bakery. Find the 20% (2 out of 10) that will have the most impact. Consider positive and negative effects.

1. cleaning the customer-facing areas of the bakery
2. doing the dishes
3. building a new menu board
4. coming up with new recipes (a fun part of the business)
5. reorganizing the pantry shelves
6. making the bank deposits
7. running ads
8. cleaning the ventilation system and other things the customers will never see

9. making the baked goods
10. browsing online for special cupcake liners and edible glitter (another fun part)

These are all tasks that can take place in a bakery. But not all of them are necessary. And some of the ones that are necessary do not need to be done every day or even every week. Say that this week, Billy Baker neglects all of these things. Which two will have the greatest impact? The answer is making the baked goods and doing the dishes. If Billy doesn't build a fancy new menu board, no big deal. But if he doesn't bake the cakes and clean the place, everyone will know it.

Those 2 items, or 20% of our list, have 80% of the impact. So be sure to identify—and do—the few things that make the most difference. As the other items really need to be done, do them, but don't allow them to take up more time than necessary.

How can you keep something from taking up more time than needed? Enter Parkinson's Law.

Parkinson's Law

Parkinson's Law, as applied in this situation, means that work will expand to fill the time allotted for it. So, if you have 12 months allotted for writing your book, the work will expand to take you 12 months. While you're doing the things that must be done, you'll notice little things that could be done. You'll do them, because you have 12 months allowed for it. If you only give yourself 12 weeks to get it done, it won't take 12 months anymore. Of course that means that you won't be making it perfect, but see above—the 80/20 Rule. You don't need to make it perfect! You just need to get it done. Yes, you'll revise it. This is just your first draft, after all. But even after you revise it, you still don't need to make it perfect. Getting it as close to perfection as possible is the job of all of your editors.

So, using Pareto's Principle and Parkinson's Law…

Decide which tasks will give you the most impact, set a time limit, and get them done. We recommend no more than two hours per day for writing your book.

Only two hours?

That's right. Feel free to keep it secret. After all, if people think you're writing your book all day, they won't put demands on your time. If they think you have four to six hours a day to waste like they do on TV, then uh-oh...

The Law of Diminishing Returns

This one may be the most important productivity principle. It says that over time, you'll get less and less benefit from what you're putting into something. It's often used in investment terms, but it absolutely applies to our efforts over time as well. Remember that the human body has limits. Our brain function declines over the course of a long stretch of work.

Say you write for 1 hour and get 1,000 words out of that hour. If you keep working hour after hour, you are not going to continue to get 1,000 words out of each hour. If you write for 5 hours straight, you might write 1,000 words the first hour, then 800, 400, 200, 100—for a total of 2,500 words that day. But if you write for 1 hour on 5 different days, you could get 1,000 words from each hour— for a total of 5,000 words. That's twice as much, and it will add up quickly. Use this law for increased productivity.

Productivity Tools

The Eisenhower Matrix

If you aren't familiar with this helpful tool, you're in for a treat. I first heard of it as "The Covey Quadrants," but it's actually called The Eisenhower Matrix. It uses two axes, two lines that represent particular aspects of any given task or project. Those aspects are importance and urgency.

It looks like this:

Every item falls into one of these four categories:

- important and urgent
- important but not urgent
- unimportant and urgent
- unimportant and not urgent

EISENHOWER MATRIX

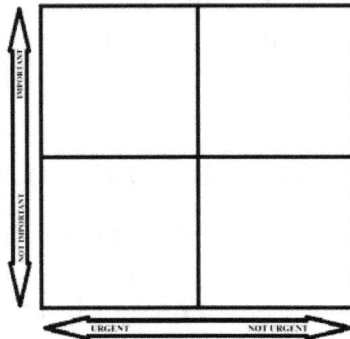

Someone approaches you with a request that needs to be completed today. That's urgent. The person is stressed out and insistent that the task is vital and simply must be done. It's important—at least to that person. But is it important to you? If it is, it falls into Quadrant 1, and that's a stove fire you have to put out. If it is not important to you, that's a Quadrant 3 item, one you delegate or decline. That might be a grease fire, but it is not in your kitchen. Quadrant 3 items really shouldn't get your time or attention.

As you probably can see right away, Quadrant 4 should never get your time and attention. This is the "Delete it" quadrant.

It is best to live in Quadrants 1 and 2, and more so in Q2.

Quadrant 2 items are the things that are important but that no one is tapping their foot waiting on. Relationships, health, and writing your book are common Q2 items.

The people who live in Q1 are the people who are constantly running around putting out fires. That's a recipe for burnout. If you find yourself there, please fix that right away. As you'll see in Chapter 6, that kind of lifestyle can kill you. My friend M.J. James, owner of The Burned Out Business Mom, can help you. Small changes can make big differences, and they can save your life.

Pomodoro Technique

The Pomodoro Technique is a "time-management" method. I don't like that term because time cannot be managed; only our actions can. That could be my neurodivergence talking, but words have meaning and are important. The technique was created by Francesco Cirillo. The name comes from the red tomato timer he used (*Pomodoro* is Italian for *tomato*).

It goes like this: The user sets a timer for 25 minutes and works as hard and as fast as possible. When the timer dings, the person takes a five-minute break. Then they do another round. After three rounds, they should take a longer break.

That's the standard Pomodoro. It can be adjusted to better fit the user's energy level and attention span. I usually do a 55–5. I recommend following The Two-Minute Rule at first. It's outlined in *Atomic Habits* by James Clear. Shift to Pomodoro later.

When you are writing your book, please start small. Set that timer for two minutes. If you're on a roll, you can keep going for a little bit.

When we get further into the book, I'll talk about turning off your inner editor/critic. Then you'll understand why I recommend starting with a bite instead of a plateful.

Idea Pantry

Similar to a home or bakery's pantry, an Idea Pantry is a place where ingredients are stored. Those ingredients might be used to make something in the future. The big difference is that the items an idea pantry holds aren't consumable or perishable. An Idea Pantry is a Word document that holds snippets of text you have written.

For years, I've been telling authors that they should never again delete anything they write. Instead, they are to cut it from their current document and paste it into their Idea Pantry.

You shouldn't be cutting anything from your manuscript while you're writing your first draft. But I know that 95% of you will.

Do it quickly and get back to work.

The more you can keep your focus on moving forward during the drafting phase, the faster you'll get your book done. Drafting = dumping. You'll refine it all later.

Routine and Rituals

The word *ritual* sounds bad to a lot of people. The word seems to be perceived as a negative thing. It's not. Humans have rituals for all sorts of things.

A ritual is something that signals to your brain that it's time to do something. Time to write, time to paint, time to sleep. Rituals are so important to productivity and creativity that the need to create at least one ritual cannot be overstated.

In the movie *Shakespeare in Love*, Shakespeare would take his quill pen in his hands and rub his palms together back and forth very quickly, then turn around in a complete circle. Only then would he start to write.

We find that to be a funny thing, kind of silly. We might say, "That's ridiculous. Why do you have to do that before the words can start to come out of you?"

But it worked for him.

I'm not suggesting that you come up with a laughable ritual, but if you want one, that's fine. Before it's time to write, say a little poem or rhyme or something. You might use candles or a diffuser, or you might eat a mint or something like that to set the tone.

Scent

Scent can be extremely powerful, and whenever people who use it as a trigger detect that particular smell, they know it's time to write.

In front of my computer monitor, I've used things like scented candles or (when it's too hot for candles) cool-mist lighted scent diffusers. When I light them up, it's time to get to work. It's not time to be on social media. It's not time to send emails to clients or prospects or anything else. Creation begins.

As soon as I put out the candles or turn off the diffusers, that is a signal to my brain that it's time to relax or otherwise switch gears.

The idea is to send a signal to your brain when it's time to produce writing and when it's okay to stop. When I do ____, I write. When I do ____, it's okay to stop writing.

At first, you probably won't notice any increase in productivity or any uptick in your willingness to do the work.

With practice, you will.

It's the way God designed our systems to work. We associate one thing with another. You sit down and light the candles. Then you write.

Over time, as you do that, when you sit down and light the candles, your brain will start producing the words.

Other triggers

You don't have to use scent. You can choose something else to use. It could be music, a particular article of clothing, or a certain chair you sit in. Some people like to keep a totem. As with ritual, this is not a bad thing. A totem is just an object that has special meaning for the person who has it.

Charles Dickens wrote with a series of porcelain figurines arranged across his desk. They were characters who kept him company as he toiled under punishing deadlines. It's not as strange as it sounds. Many of the writers I talk to keep a totem nearby as they work. It may be a small trinket or printed slogan. It's something that serves as a source of inspiration or a barrier against despair.

Whatever you use, just be consistent with it. Use it every time. It won't be long before your brain learns that the item and writing go together. Then you won't be able to help but start writing when you perform your ritual or employ your trigger. Use that to your advantage, and consciously choose what you're going to use.

Make it something you will have available any time you want to write. If it's a certain article of clothing, and you're on a trip and don't have it with you, that won't help much. But if it's a movement you make with your body, then you can write anywhere, anytime. I hope you always have your body with you.

The Myth of Multitasking

Some people say they are great at multitasking. For a long time there, it was common to see job ads demanding it: "Must be good at multitasking in a fast-paced environment."

That's a recipe for disaster, half-baked ideas, and spills all over the work space. Why do I say that?

Generally speaking, people are not doing two or more things at once. According to the American Psychological Association, people are shifting their attention. In doing so, they are losing up to 40% of their efficiency. It's even worse on tasks that take concentration.

The exception to this is a person trained in a skill called divided attention. Trainers in the PACE (Processing and Cognitive Enhancement) program have the skill and teach it. I was certified as a PACE trainer in 2015, with about 20 others. Few people can actually pay attention to two things at once.

Just do one thing at a time. Do it well. That means you should not be doing nonwriting things during your writing time. Research is not writing. Asking for endorsements is not writing. Only dumping words on the page is writing.

If you need to use apps to help you focus, do it. I've seen some that shut off users' access to social media and other websites for a set amount of time (an hour, a day). Do what you need to do so that you can focus, even if it's for just a few minutes every day.

Information about Scheduling

Every baking recipe includes time and temperature. Bake at 350 for 25 minutes, for example. The curious or impatient wonder, "What if I baked it for half the time at double the temperature?"

From experience, I can tell you that no, it does not work. You may see caramelization where you don't want it. Your baked good could have a crispy outside and a gooey inside—and not in the Chili's Molten Lava Cake kind of way.

For most recipes, you might be able to adjust the time and temperature slightly. But not by half the time and double the temperature.

What about with baking your book?

Can you take a typical pace of word count per day by the number of days, and skew it so that you can create your book faster? The answer is yes, to a point, depending on certain factors. Let's look at those factors.

Factors in how long it takes

- the length of your book
- your productivity
- your energy level
- your desire
- response time from others (interviewees, for example)
- the amount of time you have available

Length of book

The length of your book is a big factor. That alone, with all other things being equal, could halve or double the time it takes to bake your book.

To demonstrate, Aisha writes 1,000 words a day every day. If her book is 20,000 words, she'll have her first draft written in 20 days. If her book is 100,000 words, it will take her 100 days.

Productivity

If Aisha changes the number of words she writes per day, it affects how long it takes her to write her book. Dropping to 500 words per day would double the length of time it takes to write her book. If she doubles the number of words she writes per day to 2,000, it would cut the time in half. She'd have a draft in 10 days.

My time at a learning center using a metronome with the PACE program led me to believe these things:

- Each of us has a natural pace.
- With the right supports, over time, we can increase that pace dramatically.

I've seen this with writers of all types, too.

You might hear people say, "I can only write about 500 words per day. Then I go nuts."

It's okay to determine what your *current* pace of productivity is, and to either stick with it or to change it. You can only push it so far, though.

Here you'll see the baking times and temperatures above in chart form. Circle the row of figures you plan to use. Add a backup plan as well.

Note that I included the figures for a book of 50,000 words. I don't recommend that you make your first book that long.

Book Baking Chart		
Quantity	Temperature	Baking time
(word count target)	(# of words per day)	(# of days until draft is done)
20,000	250	80
20,000	500	40
20,000	1000	20
20,000	2000	10
20,000	5000	4
30,000	250	120
30,000	500	60
30,000	1000	30
30,000	2000	15
30,000	5000	6
50,000	250	200
50,000	500	100
50,000	1000	50
50,000	No More than 1,000 Words/Day	No Fewer than 50 Days

You might not want to make any of your books that long. Only make your book(s) as long as necessary.

Readers care about the results a book can help them achieve, not the heft factor.

The human body has limits. It can't go without sleep for more than three days before the hallucinations begin. It doesn't take even that long for most people. Some start to hallucinate after being up less than 24 hours, according to the National Institutes of Health. Ethics regulations control what scientists can do. They can't set up an experiment to find out how long it would take someone to die of sleep deprivation. We do know that after a few days, organ shutdown begins.

Do not get tempted to mess with your sleep for the sake of this project—or anything else, if you can help it.

You have other obligations. You can't spend every waking moment working on your book. Renting a motel room might help. My friend and client Ron Price does that when he's writing a book. Speaking of, Ron, isn't it about time for another hotel stay, my friend? Your book on burnout is desperately needed in our world today.

Energy level

Your energy level has a lot to do with how much you can write each day. So do your attention span and productivity limit. Even if your oven is constantly preheated, at some point, your brain will object. It will scream like Bugs Bunny on the Moon: "Get me outta here!"

When you do have energy, make the most of it. The following exercise will help you to chart your energy patterns. This will help you schedule your writing for times you have the most mental energy for the task. I have all of my coaching clients do an exercise I call an Energy Audit. It pinpoints the best time(s) of day and the best days of the week for you to write.

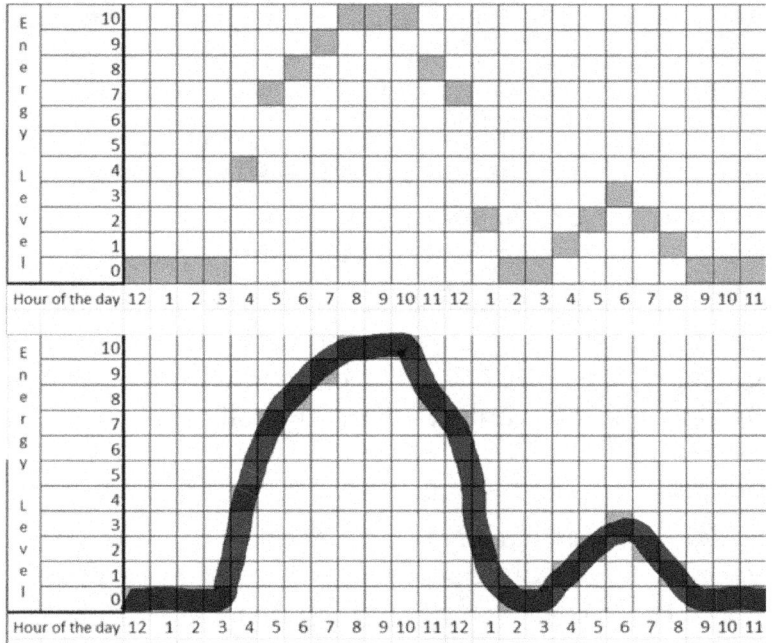

ENERGY AUDIT

Here's how you do the Energy Audit. Make sure it's a typical week for you when you do your Energy Audit. Unusual times are not good weeks to do this. Don't aim for perfection, though, either. Just pick a typical week, and do the exercise.

Set an alarm to sound at the top of the hour (8:00 versus 8:30, which is the bottom of the hour). Do that for every hour you're awake during the day. Do not disturb your sleep for this.

When the alarm sounds, take a few seconds to check in with yourself. Ask, "How mentally alert do I feel? On a scale of one to ten, how productive do I feel right now?" You could also ask yourself how productive you've been in the last hour, and chart that.

Charting

Ideally, you will chart your energy levels every day for one week. If you can't manage that, do as many days that week as you can.

Put a dot on the chart where it corresponds with that number, or fill in the square. For the hours that you're asleep, log a zero (0). Fill in one copy of the chart for each day. A copy of the Energy Audit sheet is included for you in the Resources section. A downloadable spreadsheet is at www.harshmanservices.com/YBB-book-goodies.

At the end of the full week (or as many days as you can do), add up your scores for each hour of the day for the work days. Graph them on a clean chart sheet. Then average the weekend days *separately* from the workweek days. If your Saturdays are quite different from your Sundays, skip averaging them. Look at them individually. That would give you three charts to look at.

On each of your final charts (work day average and weekend), draw a line to connect the dots or colored-in squares.

Exhaustion and pain will affect how productive you can be. If your brain feels great but your body doesn't, then chart what your body is saying. We all know that if our body wants the opposite of what our brain/mind wants, the body usually wins.

Meringue peaks

The blocks of time that are 7 and above are your peak mental energy times, or zeniths. Schedule your writing for these times if at all possible. Any stretches of time that are 3 and below are your energy troughs or nadirs. You should probably avoid trying to do things that require a lot of brain power at those times.

What about the 4–6 zone? Those times may be great for writing parts that come easily and revising your manuscript. (Revising comes *after* the first draft is complete).

Feel free to work on the more difficult parts. Please be gentle with yourself if it proves too challenging. Give yourself grace. Honor your energy cycles. Making a habit of dishonoring your body's needs and pushing through isn't noble. It's shortsighted and foolish.

After you've conducted the Energy Audit on yourself, ask yourself some questions. What patterns do you notice? Does your energy rise quickly early in the morning, stay steady, and then fizzle out by dinnertime? Does it dip after lunch, especially if you eat carbohydrates? Perhaps it rises slowly because you're not a morning person, but then it stays high for hours on end late into the night. Do you have an S-shaped curve, with two peaks and troughs?

You may have heard of these energy patterns:

- Lark
- Pigeon
- Night Owl

Or maybe you've heard of chronotypes:

- Dolphin
- Lion
- Bear

These are all attempts to classify people's energy patterns.

Each pattern has advantages, so make use of them. Do whatever you can to schedule your writing time for an energy peak.

Desire

Our level of desire affects our level of productivity and how long it takes us to do something. Say you're all fired up for a baking session. You're going to want to be in that kitchen more often than you would if a project leaves your oven cold.

Can you affect your level of desire? Yes, you can!

Here's one way. Go over your foundational questions again. Think about the people you're helping with this book. Consider the transformation they're going to be able to make during and after reading it. If that doesn't get your gas jets going, ask whether you're writing the wrong book or trying to serve the wrong people.

Now, a day or two of malaise or apathy during this process can be chalked up to the normal situation of being human. Everyone has a bad or low-energy day from time to time. If you're having more than one or two a month, you might want to see a doctor.

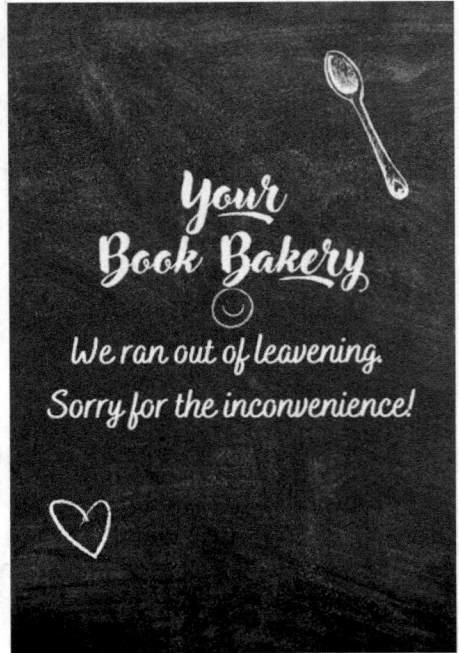

Your
Book Bakery
☺
We ran out of leavening.
Sorry for the inconvenience!

Response time

Not every book includes the stories of other people or quotations given to the author by others. Most do. For those that do, some time must be invested to gather those stories and quotations. The response time of those contributors can affect how long it takes to write your draft.

If you're interviewing people via email for your book, you'll have to wait for their responses. That could affect the time it takes to complete your manuscript. The same is true for editors and anyone else who is working on your book.

Your time available

A multitude of gurus chant in unison sayings like this:

- If it's important, you'll do it; if it's not, you'll make an excuse.
- We all have 24 hours in a day, so there's no reason you can't do it.

These are not the same:

- The 24 hours of a 45-year-old mom of three special-needs kids
- The 24 hours of an adult caregiving daughter with young children of her own
- The 24 hours of a single, able-bodied 20-year-old son who lives at home.

Anyone who denies that has problems detecting reality or is gaslighting you.

Do some people make excuses? Yes, of course.

Is it also true that there are legitimate limits? Yes.

Is it possible that there are some ways you can adjust the situation, at least for a time? Absolutely.

Temporary Adjustments

What are some of the things you might need to consider and adjust, even if temporarily?

- your standards regarding cooking and cleaning
- errands and projects
- entertainment
- your commitments, especially things others have asked you to do

We'll address each of these in turn.

Cooking and cleaning can take up quite a bit of time. There are ways to reduce that time without living like a total slob. Committees and boards will survive without you. Neighbors can find someone else to take them to appointments and on errands. If they can't, that's not your responsibility. Let's look at cooking and cleaning. These things are not likely to go away while you write your book. How can we reduce the time they take?

Needing time to write is not the only reason I developed systems to help me cut the time these things take. Nor is having children with special needs whom I homeschooled. The other big reason is I have disabilities. They affect my energy levels, pain levels, and ability to move.

When I can get things done, I get everything done that I can. Necessity led me to develop so many systems and hacks. Now you get to benefit from that.

Batch cooking

One of my favorite ways to save time (and money and energy) is to batch cook. There are many books on the topic, and you could get one. But I want you to realize that you can write your book, so I want to put everything you need in this one. For that reason, I'm including a sample menu and instructions for batch cooking a week's food.

If you like the time it saves, you're welcome to find some books on batch cooking. It's also called once-a-month cooking. Or repeat this weekly menu until your first draft is done.

This is our basic weekly menu. It has themes, if you will.

Monday: Chicken

Tuesday: Mexican (Taco Tuesday, anyone?)

Wednesday: Asian

Thursday: Italian

Friday: Seafood

Saturday: Beef

Sunday: Roast or chops of some kind

How to Batch Cook

For this sample week, I start off by soaking two types of beans overnight. One fits Mexican dishes, such as pinto or black beans. The other is a white or red bean. The next day, I get going by starting the yeast-and-sugar water for a large batch of bread. It's enough to make two loaves, one 9x13 pan, and one 10x15 pan (skip this if you don't make your own bread). I start the beans to boil and throw the chicken into the oven at 350° F.

I usually use chicken breasts, but sometimes it's thighs or a combination of both. I make one flat of chicken with no seasonings and one with seasonings. Which seasonings depends on what we're in the mood for that week. Let's say during this sample week, I'm making the following:

- roast chicken breasts and rice for Monday's dinner and Wednesday's dinner
- slicing some for a tossed salad for Tuesday's lunch and Thursday's lunch
- shredding those leftovers for chicken salad sandwiches for Saturday's lunch

On the other burners

On the other stove burners, I set to cooking a 10-lb roll of ground beef. I add a couple of chopped onions and garlic (bell peppers, too, sometimes). I make one pan Italian seasoned, one pan Mexican seasoned, and one pan with just salt and pepper added. I mix the bread dough and put it into oiled bowls and set them near the stove, covered with a tea towel.

I spread the meat onto cookie sheets to cool, and I wash the pans I used.

Then I start a big pot of rice with four cups of (dry) rice. That will be for three dinners and snacks:

- Monday with chicken
- Tuesday with pinto beans
- Wednesday with fake fried rice
- Rice pudding

Roast, rice, eggs

After that, I chop vegetables for the roast. Potatoes, carrots, celery, and onions are great for this. I throw them into the roaster or slow cooker and plop the roast on top. I shake some Badia seasoning over all of it, put the lid on, and check the rice.

Whenever the rice is done, I drain it, saving the rice milk. I spread the rice onto a cookie sheet and let the rice cool for a few minutes. Then I put it into a food container and refrigerate it. We use some of it for meals as needed. After the dinners that use it have passed, I turn the leftover rice into rice pudding. Truth be told, I often just portion out some for the rice pudding right then and make it while I'm batch cooking. When the rice milk is cool, I add some vanilla, put it in a jug or bottle, and refrigerate it.

I put on 18 eggs to hard boil. I devil six and leave the rest whole. I use the whole eggs for salads, sandwiches, and snacks. Sometimes, a few of the eggs go bad by the time we use them all, but usually, they are fine. If any do go bad, I just put them into the compost pile for the garden.

Beef and chicken

When the ground beef is cool, I divide the meat into meal-sized portions in baggies and freeze them. I don't always put dates or labels on the baggies. It's easy to see what they are (oregano or chili powder), and they'll be used that week. That meat is for Taco Tuesday, spaghetti on Thursday, and a homemade Hamburger Helper kind of meal on Saturday.

When the chicken is cooked through (no pink in it), I remove it from the oven and put bacon into the oven. I use a half sheet pan that has a rack inside it, so the bacon is lifted off of the surface of the pan, and the grease can drain. Save the bacon grease! Some of the bacon will be for breakfast on Tuesday. Some will be for adding to sandwiches, crumbling into salads, etc. The second I put the bacon into the oven, I mix up a batch of biscuit dough, pat it into a half sheet pan, and add that to the oven.

Bread

Once the bread dough has risen, I shape it into the pans. I add cinnamon sugar to one for cinnastix and let it all rise a little longer. Then I bake it until it is golden and sounds hollow when I thump it.

I stay busy the whole time, cleaning as I go and packaging each food item as it's cool enough. I also make iced tea, iced coffee/ Frappuccino drinks, and kombucha.

A week covered, mostly

One Sunday afternoon makes all of the meals for the week. Batch cooking saves so much time, fuel (electricity or gas), human energy, and money. I buy what's on sale and use it up, and buying larger packages of things often costs less per ounce. Be sure to check the per unit cost because stores can be tricky.

I don't cook the seafood ahead of time. It just doesn't keep well. Usually, we do something super simple on that night. Maybe it's baked lemon pepper tilapia or tuna noodle casserole. Once in a while, (no shame) it's fish sticks and popcorn shrimp.

Batch cooking saves time, fuel, and heating and cooling costs.

Lunches and breakfasts

Lunches are always leftovers, sandwiches, or salads. The sandwiches and salads almost always contain leftovers from dinners.

Breakfasts are also simple. On the batch-cooking day, with half of the bread dough, I make breads. With the other half, I make cinnastix (bread dough spread in a pan, cinnamon sugar sprinkled on top, and baked). I also make a giant batch of muffins or brownies and a half sheet pan with pancakes. Just pour the entire batch of batter right into the baking pan, and bake it at 350°. It can be as high as 400°, such as if it's in the oven at the same time as the bread is. Bake until golden.

After it cools, cut the giant pancake into rectangles and put them in an airtight container. It makes 20 pancakes that are about 3x4 inches. That feeds my family for at least two breakfasts and a few snacks.

If it's going to be more than two days before you eat the pancakes, freeze them once they're completely cool.

This covers breakfasts:

- pancakes on Monday
- bacon and scrambled eggs on Tuesday (use the leftover eggs for the Asian dish on Wednesday)
- cinnastix on Wednesday
- pancakes on Thursday
- muffins on Friday
- breakfast casserole on Saturday
- French toast with any leftover homemade bread on Sunday.

If your family members aren't breakfast eaters, you could use the foods for snacks, or skip making them. I do recommend bacon for sandwiches and salads, though.

Make it fun to get it done.

This gives us the following menu for the week.

WEEKLY MENU

	Breakfast	Lunch	Dinner	Snacks
Monday	Pancakes	Leftovers from last week	Roast chicken, mixed vegetables, and rice or white beans	Deviled eggs
Tuesday	Bacon and eggs	Tossed salad with chicken and hardboiled eggs	Tacos with pinto beans and rice	Homemade bread
Wednesday	Cinnastix	PB&J (or sunbutter) sandwiches	Fake fried rice with vegetables and chicken	Hardboiled eggs
Thursday	Pancakes	Taco salad with beans	Spaghetti with meat sauce and homemade bread	Cinnastix
Friday	Muffins	Leftovers	Baked lemon pepper tilapia with rice	Carrot sticks
Saturday	Breakfast casserole	Chicken salad sandwiches	Homemade Hamburger Helper with cream-of-something soup and shredded cheese	Leftovers
Sunday	French toast	Salad with crumbled bacon and the new batch of hardboiled eggs	Roast pork with vegetables	Leftovers

Even though I use recipes for books, for most foods, I don't. But here is what I do for muffins and pancakes.

Muffins (can be made gluten-free)

Dry ingredients

5 cups flour (may substitute up to 2 cups with oats, oat flour, or other flours)

4 tsp baking powder (8 if using dry additions)

1 teaspoon salt, spices to taste

½ cup dry additions: nuts, seeds, raisins, etc., optional

Wet ingredients

Up to 1 cup sugar

2 eggs

½ cup oil

2 or 3 bananas (or similar amount of other fruit—add moisture if needed to match the moisture of banana), optional

Enough liquid to make the batter the right consistency (start with 2 cups)

Mix the dry ingredients. Then add and mix in the wet ingredients. Pour the batter into a 9x13 or 10x15 baking dish to save time. When they are cooled, cut into rectangles.

If you want to make the muffins gluten-free, I recommend a cup-for-cup gluten-free flour mix.

Pancakes (can be made gluten-free)

Dry ingredients

5 cups flour (can substitute oat flour, rice flour, soy flour, etc. for some or all of the all-purpose flour)

1 TBSP baking powder

1 tsp salt

Wet ingredients

5 eggs

½ cup oil

1 cup sugar

1 TBSP vanilla extract (imitation is fine)

Enough liquid to make the batter the right consistency (3 to 5 cups)

Whisk together the dry ingredients. Then mix in the wet ingredients, adding liquid slowly until it's at the consistency you prefer. Thicker batter makes thicker, fluffier pancakes. Thinner batter makes flatter, denser pancakes. Oil the pan. Pour the batter into it, then bake at 350 until golden. Cut into rectangles and serve hot. When the remaining pancakes are cooled, put into an airtight container. Freeze if needed.

Cleaning

Can cleaning be batched as well? You bet! Rinsed dishes can be left to sit until after dinner and done all at once. The laundry can wait until the weekend. It can be batched on Saturday morning and folded and put away on Sunday evening. The floors can be done once a week, too. Just avert your eyes and tell yourself the maid will be here on Friday evening. Yeah, I know, *you're* the maid who will be there on Friday evening. You know it, too, but telling yourself that can help you get through the week. Then, when it's time to whip the house into shape, put on some music and go as fast as you can. Lower standards for a limited time will help you accomplish this dream.

Errands and projects

While it's true that some things can't wait, many can. We often deceive ourselves. We choose to believe that something is urgent and we are the only ones who can do it. Very few things require *you* to be the one to handle it, and many of those can be postponed while you work on your book. Delay and delegate as many things as you can. Remember the Eisenhower Matrix? Delay and delegate.

Entertainment

Entertainment (TV, sports, Netflix, etc.) takes up several hours a day for the average person. Each of us has to take a hard look at that and determine how much downtime is actually necessary. At the end of a 14-hour work day, I am going to hop in my bed and watch an episode of something. I won't feel one bit guilty about it! I also have to accept the consequences of my choices. A few hours a week probably won't cause any problems. If someone watches a few hours a night, that's 20+ hours they could use to write their book. Viewing time is a good place to start making cuts to carve out time for writing your book.

Now let's look at another big challenge for all the nice people. This includes people Gretchin Rubin would call Obligers. Obligers live up to other people's expectations and neglect their own. They give until their measuring cup's empty — and probably their entire flour cannister, too.

Commitments, or saying no

Whether or not you are an Obliger, you have to make time for your own projects. During this time, you will not be able to say yes to everyone. As hard as it might be, you must say no to people.

Be realistic about what you can do while you're writing your book. This means you have to acknowledge that you have work/family obligations, so you can't just write for 16 hours a day. It also means clearing off your counters so you can bake this book.

Get rid of or pause any commitments that are not life-and-death issues. I promise, everyone but tiny humans who depend on you for sustenance can make it without you for a while. Your spouse can shop and cook and clean. Your children won't die if you don't help them with school or chauffer them around. The nonprofits will find someone to handle all the things. In 12 weeks from now, you can evaluate whether to pick up any of those commitments again. You might find, as many of my students do, that you do not want to pick those things up again. You'll love the time freedom. You may realize you were doing those things not out of enjoyment but guilt. Making time to write your book can be what sets you free.

Scheduling It

Set your schedule for this project. Decide on a time of day that you'll write and for how long. Then set a backup time just in case life interferes (it has a way of doing that). Are you the kind of person who has trouble getting things done? Be sure to work with your accountability partner and/or get on the writing sprint sessions we host on Zoom. There is at least one session per day, and you may ask for other times if the slots don't work for you.

You should have some source of accountability. Once you've written for a while, you will have a better idea of how long you need to write a certain number of words.

For now, until you find out otherwise, estimate that you can write 500 words per hour. Plan for 100 hours to write your first draft.

I can show you how to outline your book in about an hour, so that part's not going to take up much time.

Remember that by changing any of the variables, you can change how long it will take you to write your first draft. The variables are how many words per hour, how many hours per week, and how many total words go into your book. Most books don't need to have 50,000 words. But we'll use that figure because it's the most commonly used cakepan.

- If you write for 5 hours each week at 500 words per hour, that's 2,500 words per week. It will take you 20 weeks to write 50,000 words of a first draft.
- If you write for 10 hours each week at 500 words per hour, that's 5,000 words per week and 10 weeks to finish your first draft.
- If you write for 5 hours a week at 1,000 words per hour, it will take you 10 weeks.
- If you write for 10 hours a week at 1,000 words per hour, it will take you 5 weeks to write a book.

Open your calendar now, please, and select the date of your deadline. Put it into the calendar. Then write that date next to your goal where you can see it constantly.

I keep my deadlines on sticky notes on the bottom of the 32-inch screen that serves as my monitor. Because it is directly in my line of sight, I see it constantly. Even when I'm not consciously aware of it, my subconscious mind is picking up on it.

You may have heard some people say it's important to write every day; others say it's not, and a third group of us say it depends. I'm in that third group.

If you need routine and function better when every day is the same, then writing daily is for you.

What if this describes you?

- You need variety.
- You go in spurts.
- You can dump chunks of a book onto a screen like a batch of bread dough onto a table.

Then join me in the "not daily" kitchen.

I have a confession to make. I'm in a group called The Daily Writer Club, led by my dear friend and client Kent Sanders, but I don't write every day. I might go a week without writing. Then I produce 15,000 words the next week on top of running my business and household. I tend to batch cook my writing. I turn out my books in a week or two, although they simmer in my brain for years or even decades. Kent knows this and is okay with it.

Only you get to decide if it serves you better to write every day. Try it. As you develop the habit, it gets easier to get the words flowing out of you. See what kind of results you can get.

What is the deadline for your goal?

Have you written it where you can see it regularly?

Break it down so you know how many words per day (on average) you need to write. Enter that number here: _____ words

Intention statement or promise to self

An intention statement differs from a goal. It helps you meet your goals by making things very clear to your subconscious and conscious mind. It needs to be specific and reasonable. It looks like this. I will [action] on [day of the week or date] at [clock time] in [location]. An example is "I will write 250 words every day of the week at 5:00 AM at the kitchen table."

Now fill in the blanks in a way that works for you:

I will _____ on _____ at _____ in/at_____.

What can you do to make yourself more accountable? Consider a commitment device.

Commitment Device

A commitment device is a way that you can pretty much force yourself to do something. In 2011, I wanted to start getting up at 4AM so I could get in a few hours of work before my children woke up in the mornings. I had discovered that the morning hours were at least twice as productive for me than any hours after noon were. Once my young kids were up, all bets were off. I might not get any work done that day. When it came to getting up early, even though I knew it was smart, I had been sporadic.

A friend had been trying to help me get up on time and had said I could call or text her when I woke up. She was in an earlier time zone, and 4AM my time wasn't an insane time for her. I hadn't been as consistent as I wanted to be, and using those hours well was important for my business.

Here's what I did to fix the situation. I wrote a check in the amount of my monthly income and made it out to the most horrendous organization I could think of. I put it in a stamped envelope addressed to that organization and put that in a larger envelope. I mailed that to my friend.

Uncracking an egg

After it was out of my hands, I called her and told her about it. "If I do not call or text you by 4AM my time, 90% of the time this month, open the envelope that is on its way to you now. Drop the smaller envelope into the mail. If I meet the goal, you shred that thing."

She was shocked, as I had told her the organization the check was made out to. She half-jokingly gasped, "Jennifer Harshman. You will go to hell if you support that organization."

"I know! That's why I have to get up on time!" And I did.

Must you threaten yourself with giving to an organization you abhor?

No.

But find *something* that will motivate you.

For some people, it's the threat of something negative. For others, it's the temptation of something sweet to them. You might want to use both the carrot cake and the whip.

Creating Your Writing Environment

Create your writing environment. This includes the physical (building, room, desk, computer) and the mental (music or quiet, working alone or with people, etc.).

If you have a home office and want to use that as your writing environment, great. If you don't have that space but want it, that doesn't mean you can't write a book. You just have to get creative.

Many a book was written at a kitchen table. Some authors love writing in coffee shops for the quiet clatter and chatter. If that's you, but you don't have the budget for all the espressos and scones, try having www.rainycafe.com running on your computer.

Some people like to sit in an armchair in their living room and write longhand into a notebook and type it up later. Or balance your laptop on your legs and go nuts.

If noise bothers you, do what you can to eliminate or reduce it.

I built a false wall in my home office to reduce the street noise. It blocked three of the windows from my view, but a lot of the noise was coming through the glass on those windows.

You might like headphones or ear plugs.

I can't stand either due to sensory issues. Instead, I use webites like Rainy Café, Brain.fm, instrumental music from YouTube, or anything else I can.

Getting up before or staying up after the other members of your household also helps many authors to get their books written. Most people who are asleep are pretty quiet.

Tools:
MS Word, Google Docs, Dropbox

When it comes to tools (as with anything else), what is obvious to some is obscure to others. Even though you probably know about these things, some people don't. Please be patient as I list the things that are needed.

A computer

To write your book, you'll need a computer. That might sound as obvious as the bakery door's bell ringing when a customer enters. It's truly not obvious to everyone. More than one person who has asked me to help them write a book did not own a computer, have access to one, or know that they needed to.

Please, for the love of chocolate cupcakes, do not write a book on your phone or tablet. It's best if you have your own computer rather than using one that belongs to a library or other location. This is true even if you get a cheap, bare-bones machine. It doesn't have to be fancy or have seven tiers. It doesn't even need to be able to access the internet. All the machine needs is the ability to run a word-processing program and perhaps connect with a printer.

Word-Processing program

You'll also need a word-processing program such as Microsoft Word. Again, what seems obvious to some is news to others. Some people swear by Scrivener; others hate it. Almost everyone has access to MS Word. Use Word.

You *could* write your book in Google Docs, but I don't recommend it. Please don't ask an editor to work on your manuscript in a Google Doc. I've done it. Never again. When a client tells me they shared their manuscript with me in a Google Doc, I say, "Great. I'll download it as a Word document, edit it, and upload it to your folder."

Storage

While I don't recommend writing or editing in them, I do recommend using Google Drive and Gmail as places to *store* your WIP (work in progress). Upload it to Drive or email it to yourself. Use that as one of your three (yes, I said *three*) places to store your manuscript.

You could also use external drives, thumb drives, flash drives, etc.

You'll want at least one of the "places" you store your WIP to be in the cloud. That way, if, God forbid, a vat of ganache floods your computer, you'll still have your book.

Tracking devices

You'll need a way to track your productivity. I recommend a timer and a calendar at minimum. Whether you use digital or analog versions of each of these is up to you. Just choose something you will use.

You might want a distraction-blocking app. In the Resources section, you'll find a paper version of a word-count tracker. You'll also find a digital version at www.HarshmanServices.com/ybb-book-goodies. I recommend using a word-count tracker of some kind. Seeing the word count growing (or not) is great motivation to continue writing your book.

Style sheet

A style sheet is a document that logs decisions you've made about your book. The style sheet for this book would include capitalizing Energy Audit. Before, during, and after you write your first draft, you'll make decisions like that. Log them in your style sheet. Then, when others work on your book, they'll be able to determine if something is intentional. If it's not on the style sheet, they can ask you about it. See the enclosed example and template in the Resources section.

Self-Awareness

You'll need to know your strengths and weaknesses when it comes to writing. Make note of any of your struggles you are aware of when it comes to writing. Do you tend to overuse a certain word/phrase? Do you use overly long sentences? These will be things to keep in mind as you write and to let your editor (and beta readers and fellow Book Bakers) know. That will help them help you.

Choose one device and one software program to use for writing. If you prefer drafting with pen and paper, that's fine, as long as you enter each day's words into your computer. I recommend using Microsoft Word, but the tool doesn't matter nearly as much as using it does. The right tool is the one you will use. Also have a way to capture the ideas that come to you when you're doing something else. Recording yourself talking into your phone is fine. Again, do whatever works for you.

Whisk Together

How will you set up your kitchen?

_____

_____

_____

_____

_____

_____

How will you use the Pareto Principle?

_____

_____

_____

_____

How will you use Parkinson's Law?

_____

_____

_____

_____

How will you use the Law of Diminishing Returns?

_____

_____

_____

How will you use the Pomodoro Technique?

_____

_____

_____

How will you use your Idea Pantry?

_____

_____

_____

_____

_____

How will you use routines and rituals?

_____

_____

_____

_____

_____

_____

_____

If you haven't already done so, make marks on the Book Baking Chart. What's your plan?

Do your Energy Audit.

List ten things that it would be possible for you to temporarily pause.

_____

_____

_____

_____

_____

_____

Commit to three.
Circle them.

Chapter 5: Safety in the Kitchen (Warnings)

This is the hardest chapter for me to write, and probably for you to read. Why? It contains the negatives, the things to watch out for. I'll keep it as short as I can, and I'll try to knead some leavening into it to lighten it up.

Fire Damage

Self-care is covered in the next chapter, so I'm not talking here about burning out. I'm talking about opening yourself up to fire damage from others.

Hot Topics

Instead, I want to encourage you to be careful regarding what you say in your book and in any materials that are in connection to your book or other platforms. This includes social media platforms. Some subjects can be risky:

- abortion
- capital punishment
- class warfare and oligarchy
- disability
- discrimination
- drugs and medications of any kind
- education, including school reform, school choice, homeschooling
- The Electoral College
- environment
- federal vs state
- free-market capitalism
- government actions, including mandates, taxes, unconstitutional agencies, and more
- gun control
- healthcare

- immigration
- law enforcement
- livable wage
- marriage, family, parenting morality
- origin of the universe
- patriarchy/ sexism/rape culture

- politics
- privacy rights
- religion
- social problems of any kind
- student debt
- vaccines

Some people even get their dander up about pet ownership, believe it or not. The list of things people choose to get upset about would make a book all by itself. These are the common ones in the US.

I'm not saying that you shouldn't take a stand on any of those things or write a book about any of them. Just be aware that you might bring down the wrath of those who play God with the lives of people who don't bow to them.

Imagine a giant vat of syrup exploding all over you. You might make it out of that situation, but it's going to take a while to get cleaned up.

Choose wisely.

Even if you avoid all those sticky things, you will still run into problems.

Food critics

Anywhere you "put yourself out there," you will encounter critics and haters. Although a person can be both, they are not the same thing. Critics can point out things that actually could be improved. Sometimes they deliver lemon juice or tart cherries when you were hoping for sugar or honey. If used well, the lemon juice and tart cherries can make a cheesecake great! Haters, on the other hand, can be like mold in the butter if we let them.

Mold on any soft food sends runners deep into that food and is impossible to remove. It makes the food unsafe to eat.

On the Platform Launchers call one night, owner, author, and podcaster John Stange said this about haters: "Their only purpose is to destroy." It reminded me of mold.

Detach yourself emotionally whenever you get feedback on anything you've created. Choose some things you can say to yourself when someone burns you. Here are some ideas:

- "Everyone has an opinion, and that doesn't harm me."
- "I am not for everyone, and that's okay."
- "There is probably some truth in that, and it's my job to find it."
- "They care enough to speak up, and I appreciate that."

Thank everyone for the feedback whether they are fans, dispassionate, or haters. Thank them whether you like it or not, agree with it or not, and choose to make use of it or not. Remember that no matter the source, feedback could help you make your book the best it can be.

Think about what you can say because you're going to practice it later in this chapter. Here are some ideas:

- "Thank you for letting me know."
- "Thank you. I'll take that under advisement."
- "I have given this some thought, and you have a good point. Thank you for bringing it up."
- "You seem passionate about this, and it's an important topic/problem/idea. Thanks for sharing how you feel."

You'll also face other obstacles.

- Writing your book will present challenges.
- You'll get tired of writing sometimes.
- A TV show will look so tempting, and you'll want to skip your writing session "just this once."
- Or you'll want to stay in your warm and comfy bed with your marshmallow pillow. Just this once.

These things rarely end up happening just once. Refer to the sections on focus. Persist. You can do this!

Okay, now it's time for a harsh truth.

Uncaring and Disinterested

Unless the people already know and love you, they probably don't care about you or your book. Most humans only care about what your book (and you, via your book and other offers) can do for them. Saints are selfless, but there aren't many of those walking around these days.

Positioning your book well answers the question that is in every reader's mind:

"Why should I read this book?" In other words, "What's in it for me?"

If you don't know the answer to that question before you start writing your book, you may write a book that serves no one.

Let people know right away what your book will do for them. You can make a promise in the title and subtitle, as this book does: *Your Book Bakery: Making it easy to write a book.* Here are some more examples that make a promise in the title/subtitle:

5,000 Words Per Hour: Write faster, write smarter by Chris Fox

Feast and Famine No More: How to fill your editing schedule and keep it full by Blake Atwood

How to Talk so People Listen by Sonya Hamlin

$1,000 100 Ways by Nick Loper

Conquer the Entrepreneur's Kryptonite by James Woosley

What to Expect Regarding Book Sales

Nothing. Have no expectations.

Does that mean that you will sell zero books? Not necessarily.

Does it mean you should do no book marketing because you might not sell any books? No.

Sometimes, my job is to be the bearer of bad news or what sounds like it. It can leave people with a sour taste in their mouths. I'll do my best to make this quick and get to the good news.

The "bad news" is that most books sell fewer than 300 copies in their lifetime. If you're in this because you hope your income from book sales will be richer than Bavarian cream, this might not be the kitchen for you. You might want to go write romance novels and make marketing them your full-time job.

You probably won't get rich from selling your nonfiction book. Not directly, anyway. Use it as a door opener. Have the right expectations, and you'll feel successful.

Jennifer! If I'm not going to sell many copies of my book, then how can I feel successful? Why would I even write this book?

I'm so glad you asked. It's connected to the good news.

You're writing it because it helps people and opens doors for you to help more people—and get paid to do so.

My clients' typical keynote speech brings them $10,000. How many of those would they need to line up to make a comfortable income? Most say a dozen a year. That's one a month. Say it takes you a full workday to line up that one presentation a month. What could you do the other 19 workdays in every month?

I bet you could offer coaching, build a membership, create a course, make a workbook or journal to go with your book, or start any of several other streams of income. All because you wrote your book.

Does that sound sweeter?

Writing Groups

What are writing groups? Should I join one? What are the pros and cons to a writing group?

Writing groups (in person or virtual) aim to provide support. They come in many flavors and tiers of quality and price.

The pros of participating in a group include accountability, coaching, and support. A good group will provide resources and help you stay on track with your writing and submissions.

The cons:

- It could be the blind leading the blind.
- It could cost more than it should.
- It could be led by a shady character or
- It could have some members who are con artists who prey on other members.

The most common negative to a writing group is that it doesn't help you improve your writing. I don't know about you, but to me, that is a waste of time.

By all means, get involved with a writing group. Be careful. Make sure it's not too expensive. The leader does have to make a living and maintain the website if there is one, so a fee is reasonable. Make sure it's actually going to help you. Even a good writing group might not be the best fit for a particular writer. Don't feel bad about moving on and finding the one that is right for you. Your Book Bakery: 12 Weeks to a manuscript is a writers group you can trust. I also highly recommend The Daily Writer Club. It's led by my dear friend, referral partner, and client Kent Sanders. He is a former professor and is now a full-time professional writer and ghostwriter.

On a related note, I have two recommendations if you're interested in any of these:

- podcasting
- blogging
- speaking
- coaching
- creating courses

The recommendations are the 48 Days Eagles community and Platform Launchers.

See the Your Book Bakery book goodies page at Harshman Services for links and special deals.

Citing Sources

Citing your sources is simply saying where you got the information. Citation is extremely important. Remember that stealing is bad.

For now, all you need to know is that if you say something in your book that is not common knowledge or from your personal experience, you need to say where you got that information. This can keep you from being sued.

While you're researching, just capture the source in some way. Many people prefer to grab screenshots. Later, to put them in proper form, you can use Citation Machine online. Be sure to use the Chicago tab. Citing sources helps you avoid committing copyright infringement.

Copyright Infringement

What is copyright infringement, and why is it worse than putting rotten eggs in a cake?

The people who ask this are people who haven't created much (or anything) yet. Because once you have created, you won't want it to be stolen. Sooner or later, someone will steal it.

I will never forget the first time I found out that someone had stolen one of my articles.

Picture it. I was sitting at the computer, facing east. There was a stack of papers and clutter all over the desk, and an ashtray right in front of me (yes, I used to smoke).

My editor at Suite101 told me to do Google searches for my article titles to check for plagiarism of my work, so I did.

Stolen recipes

I had just conducted a search. What came up at the top of the search engine results pages (SERPS) was not my article. Well, it *was* my article, but it didn't have my name on it as it should have.

I said, "What the…?" and clicked on it. I didn't know I was probably paying the thief by doing so. Many earn from traffic, so the more people see it, the more the thief gets paid.

Later, I did know that I was probably paying the thief by clicking through to the article. I didn't care. I had to be sure each piece was mine so I could do something about it. The thief wouldn't get paid for my article for long.

Sure enough, it was my article. My eyesight changed. That stack of clutter? I couldn't see it. Neither could I see the rest of the room. My vision zoomed in like a psychotic camera with a will of its own. All I could see was that computer screen, with *my* article on some thief's site!

Adrenaline surged. My hands shook and my heart raced. I had to do something about it. I immediately began a frantic Google search about what to do. Thank God for Google, as I often say (even though I don't like their monopoly or big-brother-like powers).

I read and read, and chain smoked a few cigarettes while I found out what to do. By the time I got out of that chair, I had filed my first DMCA (Digital Millennium Copyright Act) notice. I could also see properly again.

Within hours, my work was once again mine, and that entire website had been shut down. "Freaking thief," I said, perturbed but relieved.

There were many other instances of people stealing my work. I sometimes got a little riled over it but nothing like the first time. Now, it's old hat. I just file a DMCA and go on with my day.

Guard your cookies

Don't let people get away with swiping your work. That said, there is such a thing as fair use. It can also be argued that there really isn't anything completely new and original anyway. Everything comes from something else.

That may be true. But a writer presents something in a certain way, reflecting his/her style and own way of wording things. That *can* be stolen, and it is still wrong to steal. So don't use anything from anyone without permission—always err on the side of caution, and ask.

I have had great success when I've asked for permission to quote people or use part of their work in the classroom. Most people are honored and thankful that you ask.

Teachers are the worst copyright infringers and thieves in the world. I say that unapologetically as a teacher. They are not supposed to show movies in the classroom unless the copyright owner allows it. They should not copy parts of books without written permission from the publisher.

Some books are intended to be photocopied for worksheets and such. I'm not referring to those.

When I wrote Penguin asking for permission to use a section of one of their books in the classroom, they granted it. They also told me that I was the first teacher to ask but that many teachers photocopied and used it anyway. That's sad.

What You Can Do about Infringement

If you know someone's infringing on the copyright of another, what can you do? You could tell the person to stop, then notify the copyright holder. Or you could just notify the copyright holders. What the owners of the works choose to do about it (which may be nothing) is up to them. You can educate others about copyright infringement, especially any children you know. Even kids know stealing is wrong, and reaching children can create a sea change in society.

If you find your work online used without your permission or in a way you didn't allow, you can do something about it. You can file a DMCA notice. The internet service providers do not want to be shut down. That is what can happen if they allow infringing material to be on sites they host. They will act swiftly to get that stolen piece taken off their servers. Over the course of a few years, I filed 50 DMCAs. None of the swiped copies of my work stayed up more than 36 hours after I filed. Most were gone within a few hours. That is satisfying. It is only a matter of time—especially if you write online—until someone steals your work.

"Do I need to copyright my work?"

This is one of the most misunderstood issues in the field of writing and publishing. When you tell someone that you're writing something, they say, "Be sure to copyright it!" First, the correct phrase is "copyright protect it." Second, every creative work (music, writing, painting) is *automatically* copyright protected. *The creator* owns the copyright.

There is a process to ensure that it is *clear* that you own the copyright, though. That process is to register your copyright with the US Copyright Office (as of 2022, there is a $65 fee for each work).

If you write online, you'll want to protect your content there as well. Back up your website(s) and protect them from hackers the best you can.

Being sure you don't infringe

Don't be a thief. Be an honest and honorable writer. And if you ever teach, be sure to get written permission before you use something.

It's simply the right thing to do. You're an author, and you don't want someone stealing your work, so don't misuse anyone else's, either. Golden Rule and all that. This means citing your sources and making sure that you have the legal right to use every image in your book.

You can also be sure that the people involved with producing your book do not commit copyright infringement. Be sure your cover designer doesn't use images they shouldn't. If you're working with a SPAA, that should be addressed in your contract. The agency should ensure that their designer uses only images that are allowed.

The rights over song lyrics and poems are staunchly defended. Do not use either without written permission from whichever person or entity holds the rights to the song or poem. Some people try to claim Fair Use Doctrine on this. That works for quoting portions of books and other works but not for songs and poems. Anything that even brings to mind the work can be considered infringement. Yikes.

There is a misconception that you can't use names of products or the titles of books or songs in your book. This is false. You can mention these things. That is not copyright infringement. If you mention them in a positive or neutral light, you'll probably have nothing to worry about. It's only if you trash talk them that you might have to worry about a defamation suit.

Defamation

Defamation is when someone's words end up causing harm to another entity's reputation or livelihood. Libel and slander sit under the umbrella called defamation. They are related but not the same thing.

Both are spreading lies about another entity (person or company). Libel is when the words are printed. Slander is when the words are spoken.

There is a misconception that if you say anything negative about someone, they can sue you for defamation. Generally speaking (again, I'm not a lawyer, and this is not legal advice), it has to be false. If you say something negative that is true, the person isn't going to win that lawsuit. But consider this: do you want to hire a lawyer to defend you if you were to be sued?

The answer to that should guide you.

Beware

I wish I could say that author scams were rare. I can't. For every good guy out here who wants to help you, there are nine who want to take your cake and eat it, too. These are some things you should look out for and stay far away from.

Vanity presses

Vanity presses, even those connected to a traditional publisher, will eat everything in the bakery, follow you home, and clean out your pantry there, too. A vanity press charges authors to publish their books, but they don't really do anything other than print a run of books. The author has to buy the entire run, of course. The vanity publisher won't try to sell them. The author has a garage full of books. The books don't sell because they weren't edited and the covers stink.

In recent years, some big traditional publishers decided to hop on the vanity press gravy train. I lost all respect for them in that moment. There may be more of them, but these are the ones I became aware of.

- Archway (Simon and Schuster)
- Westbow Press (Harper Collins and Author Solutions, a major scammer according to many sources)
- Westbow Press (Thomas Nelson—Wait a minute! Isn't Westbow Press the baby of Harper Collins and Author Solutions? Yeah. How's *that* for confusing?)
- Balboa Press (Hay House)

Some vanity presses operate under more than one name. Some of those use more than one name at the same time. Others just change their name after they get caught defrauding enough people to bake up a bad reputation. The smell reaches enough authors that the flow of honey toward the vanity press starts to dry up, so the scammers just change their signage and keep on. Here are some other vanity presses, according to Victoria Strauss of the Science Fiction and Fantasy Writers Association:

- America Star Books (formerly PublishAmerica)
- American Book Publishing
- Archebooks Publishing
- Artemis Publishers, Ltd
- Ashwell Publishing, d/b/a Olympia Publishing
- Austin Macauley Publishers
- Commonwealth Publications
- Minerva Press Ltd., a UK vanity publisher with branches in India and the USA
- Northwest Publishing
- Oak Tree Press
- Park East Press (formerly Durban House, formerly Oakley Press)
- Pegasus Elliot Mackenzie Publishers Ltd.
- Press-Tige Publishing, owned by Martha Ivery (who also operated under an alias as a fee-charging literary agent)
- PublishAmerica
- Raider Publishing International, also d.b.a. RPI Publications (former names include Green Shore Publishing, Purehaven Press, and Perimedes Publishing)
- Sovereign Publications, owned by Deering Literary Agency
- SterlingHouse Publisher, also d/b/a as International Book Management (Pittsburgh, PA–imprints include, among others, Pemberton Mysteries, 8th Crow Books, Cambrian House Books, Blue Imp Books, Caroline House Books, Dove House Books, and PAJA Books)
- Strategic Book Publishing and Rights Agency (SBPRA)/ Publish On Demand Global (PODG) (formerly known as Strategic Publishing, Strategic Book Group, Eloquent Books, The Literary Agency Group, and AEG Publishing Group)
- Tate Publishing & Enterprises, a self-styled Christian publisher based in Oklahoma
- Vantage Press

It's likely that there are many more. And, as you can see, they often change their names. They pop up all the time. Be careful.

Self-Publishing assistance agencies

Vanity presses shouldn't be confused with self-publishing assistance agencies (SPAA). A SPAA provides valuable services. Not all offer every one of these services, so be sure you know what you're paying for:

- developmental editing
- line editing
- copy editing
- interior design
- layout/formatting
- cover design
- proofreading
- book positioning
- keyword research
- assistance in uploading to Amazon and other platforms
- book marketing advice
- promotion

Also be aware of the value of the various elements. About twice a week, someone will contact me to ask my opinion on an offer they received from a vanity press, hybrid publisher, or SPAA.

Here's just one example.

An author found my website and got onto my calendar for a "pick my brain" session to ask me about two offers she'd received. One was from someone claiming to be a traditional publisher. The other was from someone who said they'd help her upload her book to Amazon.

First, let's look at the one who claimed to be a traditional publisher.

This person wanted $10,000 from her to publish her book, and on top of that, she'd have to buy 5,000 copies of her book from them at retail (That's an additional $80,000 in profit to them).

Ladies and gentlemen, that is a vanity press.

Are you choking? It gets worse.

Come to find out, this is all they offered to do for her:

They would format her manuscript, upload it to Amazon and their own website, and "work their magic" so bookstores could buy it.

She would be responsible for finding and hiring the editors and cover designer, and paying for all of that herself. (A traditional publisher handles and pays for all of the editing, designing, and more.)

Okay, so let's look at the things they would do for her for $10,000 and the common prices for each.

They would format her manuscript. (Under $1,000)

They would create a cover for her book. (Under $1,000 — usually far under that)

They would upload it to Amazon and their website. (Anyone can do this themselves, but the price we've commonly seen for assistance is $200 if the author has done the keyword research and category research themselves and $1,200 if the provider does it. The vanity press did not offer to do the research.)

They would get her book listed with a book wholesaler so that bookstores can order it. (An author can do that themselves. In fact, simply uploading the book to IngramSpark does that. How sneaky of that person to imply that they do some hard work there.)

Added up, they charge authors several times the actual value of the service they provide. On top of that, they lied to her at least twice:

- "We are a traditional publishing house."
- "Only a traditional publisher can get your book into bookstores."

I really don't know how some people sleep at night.

The other offer she'd received had a much smaller price tag but wasn't much better. It was from someone who said he would help her upload her book to Amazon. No editing. No formatting. No cover. No research. Just uploading to Amazon. There's nothing wrong with offering a limited and specific service. Here's where the problem comes in.

He said it would cost her four thousand dollars.

I spelled that out instead of using numerals just in case you might think there was a typo in the digits. Four. Thousand. Dollars. That's a lot of cookies.

For about an hour of his time.

If he were to upload on a day when Amazon is being glitchy, it might take him a full day or even two of checking from time to time to see if the platform is done "thinking" and ready to move to the next step. But still. Four thousand bucks? No way.

As I said, I don't know how some people sleep at night.

If you, too, would like my unbiased, professional opinion on something, you're welcome to schedule a "pick my brain" session as well. Just go to https://calendly.com/jennifer-harshman/consult, make your payment, and pick a time that works for you.

I want to be clear: This is not some trick to get you to hire me. Plenty of editing business flows to me from referrals thanks to the hundreds of authors who loved my work on their books. The only reason I do these consults is because I hate seeing authors get hurt. It's why I started this business in the first place.

"Agents" who approach you

Unless you're famous, no legitimate agent is going to approach you. Real agents have plenty of authors approaching *them*, and they spend all their time selling their clients' books to publishers.

"Publishers" who approach you

Same as above. If someone claiming to be a publisher contacts you, especially via social media or email, they're a scammer. No real publisher has the time or need to go hunting for authors. They're busy wading through their slush pile and stacks of book proposals. If someone contacts you pretending to be a publisher, the safe thing to do is to report and block them.

Obscure writing contests

Preying on the aspirations of budding authors and other writers, some people create fake contests and raffles.

Do your due diligence. When you hear of a contest, look it up online. Go to sites like Writers Digest, VictoriaStrauss.com, and The Write Life. See what they have to say about what to look for regarding contests in general. They might even have the particular one you're curious about on their no-go list.

Contracts with publishing houses

Suppose you do pursue traditional publishing. You find and hire an agent. The agent attracts the interest of a publishing house. It's tempting to get all excited and sign that contract.

Don't.

Take it to a lawyer who specializes in publishing contracts and represents authors (not publishing houses).

Why?

The publisher is looking out for their own interests, and you need people at that table who are looking out for *yours*. This is why you really need to have a lawyer look over every contract.

Whisk Together

Go back to the list of hot topics. Lightly draw a line through any that you know you want to avoid in your book, blog posts, etc.

If there are any that you're set on using, are you prepared to be covered in syrup? If so, circle those topics.

Prepare for the food critics.

Write out three things you will say to yourself when criticism comes.

_____

_____

_____

_____

_____

_____

_____

Write out some things you'll say to critics when their words sting.

Write out some things you'd like others to say when you need encouragement.

_____

_____

_____

_____

_____

_____

_____

_____

_____

_____

_____

_____

Chapter 6: Self-Care While Writing a Book

On Not Dying

Taking good care of yourself is important. You don't want to end up in a room full of sad doctors who say, "You need five organ transplants. We can't get you on a single list because needing that many organs makes you a terrible risk. Go home. Make your funeral arrangements, and kiss your babies goodbye. You have a day or two to live, and there is nothing anyone can do for you. We're sorry."

That is what happened to me after 30 years of extreme overwork *and* stress. That was in 2006. Now, I warn others of the danger of pushing themselves too hard for too long and of heavy stress loads.

You can't bake around the clock (overwork). You shouldn't put up with 42 customers in your store yelling for sweets (stress). And you can't make 42 different desserts at once (overwork and stress).

Concept of Self-Care

Perhaps you've heard some negative ideas surrounding the concept of self-care.

- Wasting half their annual income on a vacation (when they can't afford anything)
- Dumping an entire paycheck on a purse or briefcase (and neglecting the utility bills)
- Blowing the grocery budget for their family of five on a spa day (making their family suffer)

These are *not* what I'd call good examples of self-care. Those people are being irresponsible.

Self-care does not have to be extravagant. In fact, it doesn't even have to cost any money at all. True self-care is more about giving oneself a break to recuperate, recreate, and rejuvenate. Another thing I want to make clear is that done right, self-care isn't selfish.

When you're baking your book, I want you to take extra-good care of yourself. Sleep more. Drink pure water. Find silence. Use music judiciously. Sometimes you'll need relaxing music, and other times, you'll need something to get your ovens going.

This is one of the most important things in this book, so please remember it. Every day from now until one month after your book is published, do at least three self-care activities:

- Sleep all your body wants.
- Drink pure water (some with added electrolytes so you don't disrupt your sodium balance).
- Add one of your choosing.

Self-Care Activities

Below, you'll find a list of some examples of self-care activities. Only you get to say what feels like self-care to you, so you may pick from this list, or come up with items of your own. Just remember to select things you can afford (in money and time) to do. We don't want you saying, "Oh, I can't do that one this week because of my budget." Uh-uh. It doesn't have to be a three-layered cake. Maybe it's a mini muffin.

Pray or meditate to rest your mind.	Get a massage, Feldenkrais, or other bodywork.
Go for a walk.	Rub peppermint lotion on your feet.
Listen to music.	
Take a bath.	Do some gentle stretching.
Have a cup of tea or other warm beverage.	Get in a hard workout.
	Journal or talk to a friend.
Take a nap or go to bed early.	Book an extra counseling session.

Sit in the park or other public place and smile at nature, children, and dogs.

Verbally list things you're grateful for.

Go horseback riding.

Stargaze from a warm location.

Watch a video of a fire or flowing water.

Eat a salad or other light, nourishing food.

Cheer yourself and others on because you're doing something wonderful, and it's going to change the world.

Rewards

Ordinarily, reading is a great reward. I suggest Your Book Bakery participants skip using anything with words as a reward for making progress on their books. I tell them, "If you do read, I hope you choose marshmallow fluff."

As with self-care activities, only you can say what is a reward for you. Here's a list to get the ideas flowing. Feel free to choose your own.

music

scented candles

adult coloring books

horseback riding

a Sunday drive

candy

a tube of acrylic paint

a new pen

stationery

a disco ball

going roller skating

watching a movie

a new shirt

a new pair of shoes

sleeping in

takeout

a gym membership

having a party

Choose three rewards you'll give yourself:

- a small one you'll partake of every day that you work on your book (a metaphorical cookie, if you will)
- a medium-sized reward you'll indulge in once a week (a fictional donut)
- and one large treat you'll give yourself at the end (the proverbial cake)

Here are the icons that represent them:

Just as only you can say what's a reward for you, only you can decide which things are small, medium, and large rewards.

On the book resources page, you'll find printable tracking sheets you can download, print, and use. You'll also find links to stickers that work well with the sheets. Use the stickers to track the days you work on your book. Reward yourself daily, weekly, and at the end of your first draft.

Whisk Together

Select ten self-care activities that interest you. Write them here.

_____ _____

_____ _____

_____ _____

_____ _____

_____ _____

Commit to practicing three of them daily. Which ones did you choose?

_____

_____

_____

Select ten rewards that interest you for daily rewards. Write them here.

Commit to giving yourself one small reward each day. You may use them more than once. Keep track of which ones make you feel the best.

Select ten rewards that interest you for weekly rewards. Write them here.

Commit to giving yourself one medium-sized reward each week.

Select five rewards that interest you for your "I finished my first draft!" reward. Write them here.

_____

_____

_____

_____

_____

Choose one. Which is it?

_____

Part Three
Baking Your Book:
Writing your first draft

Chapter 7: Outlining and Planning Your Book

Every project needs planning if it is to go well. Sewing, hosting, redecorating, traveling—all of these undertakings should have a plan.

You can plot some of those activities in minutes. Others take much longer. Some can be done solo, and others might involve a family member or friend. Building a house takes extensive planning and many meetings with the architect, builder, and others. It takes several months or even years. Baking your book only requires a few meetings—one or two with an agency owner, and the rest with yourself.

Note: If you choose to work with several providers instead of a one-stop shop, you'll have one or two meetings with each person. That looks more like building a house. A one-stop shop will definitely and dramatically reduce the time the planning takes you.

Either way, you'll need to do some planning yourself. When you meet with yourself to plan your book, you'll do several things:

- Draft your answers to all of the foundational questions.
- Decide what goes into your book and what should be saved for another book or for blog posts, social media content, etc.).
- Delineate where the material should go in your book.
- Designate the tone for your book.
- Determine the positioning of your book.
- Deign to use glyphs, callout boxes, backgrounds, images, or any other visual components desired. (This can be done after your manuscript is written.)

Creating an Outline

Oh, no. Did I just use the dreaded O word? Yes. Yes, I did. But don't worry. I'll turn that into a more palatable process, too.

Outlining nightmare

Index cards are everywhere, with disjointed notes on them. A blank sheet of paper that is supposed to be your completed outline is threatening to tell the teacher on you. The teacher is standing in front of you, slapping the palm of her hand with a ruler. You're next.

Perhaps it's been years since you've been in school, but you can still remember moments of stress.

It's no wonder so many people hate outlining.

"Pantsers" are people who write by the seat of their pants and refuse to use outlines. "Plotters" plan their writing before they begin. Pantsers are more common than plotters.

I firmly believe that the pain we went through in school has a lot to do with that. Intended or not, teachers contribute to people's hatred of outlines. Many people have a hard time thinking in that linear way. The unsavory experience left most of us with a burned-cookie taste in our mouth for writing.

Creatives and leaders tend to be more "right-brained" or more big-picture, holistic thinkers. This group has a harder time with traditional outline structuring. That is a "left-brained," detailed, linear-thinking activity. (I put those into quotation marks because some debate whether left/right brained is real.)

Preventing a burn

Outlining doesn't have to be scary or painful. If you change what you think about outlining, it can become easier and painless. Perhaps do it in a couple of different ways.

The purpose of outlining is organization. One can achieve organization in more than one way.

Mind maps or other graphic organizers can be helpful. So can index cards (No, not the dreaded index cards!), but not the way they taught us to use them in school. You don't need to put citations or mile-long sentences on your cards. That just makes things complicated, and there's no need for that.

Thank God, there is more than one way to position your ingredients on the countertop. Mind mapping is a fabulous first step. Turning that mind map into a functioning (note I did not say traditional) outline is easy. First, let's talk about mind mapping and do that with your book.

Mind Mapping

Mind mapping is a visual way of organizing information on paper (or white board or screen). It can be done "out of order" or in a nonlinear way. It's excellent for right-brain or holistic thinkers. Many Creatives are "right-brain thinkers" and find mind maps helpful for organizing ideas. In an email to my special subscribers, I explained mind maps and mentioned a free mind map starter sheet. Here are the simple steps for using a mind map.

Write the title or topic in the shape in the middle. Write one main aspect of that topic in another shape. Repeat as many times as needed. If you run out of shapes and need more, just add more. It's okay to grab another sheet of paper or to print many copies of the free mind map starter sheet below. On the lines, write down the details or minor aspects. Your mind map does not have to be neat or pretty. Just keep thinking of things and writing them on your paper.

Here are the steps in mind mapping.

1.

2.

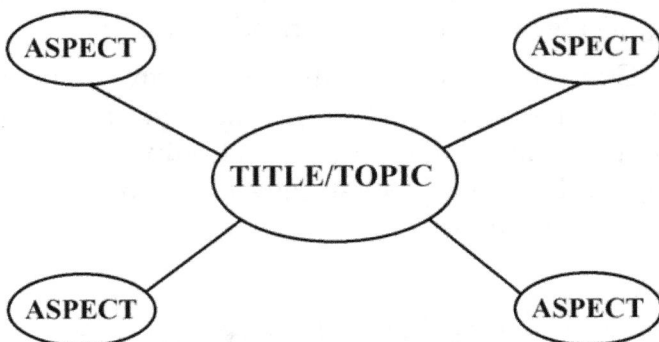

3.

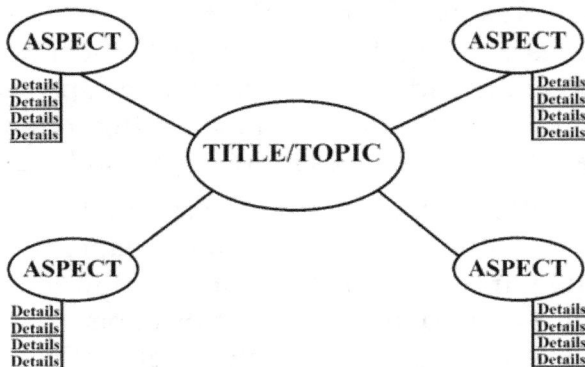

In the Resources section, you'll find a link to a downloadable, printable mind mapping sheet.

You can then turn your mind map into an outline for your book.

On my website, there are some videos to walk you through creating an outline. These help whether you can jump straight into that linear structure of a traditional outline or need a couple of steps to get there.

You may be a "right-brained" or more holistic or nonlinear thinker. You may see the big picture rather than a straight line.

Perhaps you think associatively, as many do. One thing may remind you of another idea. Then that one leads to something else. By the end, you (or others) may wonder how you got there.

If these sound like you, then try mind mapping. Give yourself plenty of room on the page, and whip up something cool.

Combining Two Worlds

For years, I wrote hundreds of pages of online content. A huge part of that was search engine optimization (SEO). That's creating pieces of writing in such a way that it would show up well in search engine results pages (SERPS). To be effective, I had to learn all about keyword research. Then I had to conduct it for every article and website page and structure the pieces to fit what the data called for. I had to serve the people doing the online searching, too.

What is keyword research?

Keyword research is one of those things that you can learn (the basics of) in a day, and yet take years to master. It tells you what Internet users are searching for—what they are typing into search engines. Some are only looking for information, not intending to buy anything. Most people today do use the Internet to find things to buy—more than 80% of people alive now, last I heard. See: https://www.invoca.com/blog/retail-marketing-statistics.

Knowing what people are searching for lets you know what products or services (or writing topics) are hot. It's a way to go to your audience and ask them what they want to read, so you can write it for them. It gives you a huge advantage over other writers. One of my specialties (my favorite hobby, one might say) is KWR. You can learn to do it yourself or hire someone else. It's totally up to you. I include it free for my clients.

Keyword research and outlines

Did you know that you can use KWR to tell you what needs to go into your nonfiction book?

People in all fields would be wise to use KWR, but especially website and business owners and writers. Good KWR helps you know what to write about.

Believe it or not, it can practically write your outline for you.

How much is your time worth?

If it's more than a couple of dollars an hour (whose isn't?), then you'd be better off to have someone else do the research for you.

While helping authors for decades, I combined the world of SEO and book creation. You can see what overlapping the two fields allowed me to do:

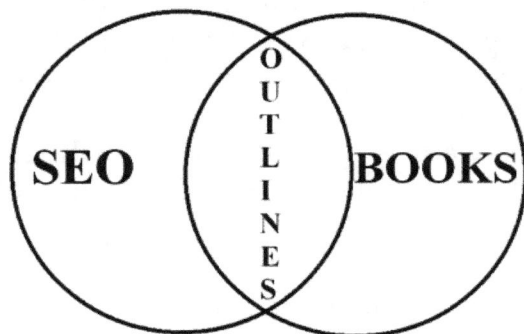

Everyone who learned of it was incredulous and then thought it was ingenious. I didn't realize how special it was. That's the way it goes: what comes easily to one person is amazing to others. Later, I added personal productivity to create my Blue Ocean.

How to outline using keywords

I help people create their outlines all the time. One of the first things I do is conduct KWR on their topic/title. The information gives me what I need to create the outline or Table of Contents for their book. I examine the keywords that have a good demand ranking and are broad enough to make a suitable segment of the book. Then I put them into a sensible order that will take the reader from Point A to Point B.

More specific keywords go under those chapter headings. I see the patterns and organize the data into the outline.

This process takes all the pain away from the author. The author might want to tweak the outline a bit, but the majority of what they need is right there.

Outlining tools

I recently explained to a client the process I use to outline books. She told me about something a character said in *The Matrix*. "He said when he was looking at all the zeroes and ones scrolling down his screen, he didn't see digits anymore. All he saw was redhead, blonde, etc. That's what *you* do: you see the patterns in the data and pull out the outlines for our books. That's an amazing superpower. I could never do that, and I'm a data scientist."

I told her she could in fact do it herself. All she needed was the right tools. You can use the same things to do it yourself. My favorite tool for this is the Brainstormer at Site Build It. At the time of this writing, it costs about $400 a year (The WordPress version is substantially less).

My affiliate link for Solo Build It! is http://www.sitesell.com/Jennifer360.html

My affiliate link for SBI! for WP is http://sbiwp.sitesell.com/Jennifer360.html

Letting SEO write your outline

To be sure you have all of the ingredients you need for your book, you'll need to do some research. Specifically, you need to conduct KWR and a literature review.

	Keyword	demand	supply	profitability
1	Keyword	demand	supply	profitability
2	leadership	155928	321952	484
3	leadership quotes	104204	48082	2167
4	servant leadership	54482	15126	3601
5	leadership styles	51975	8098	6418
6	leadership definition	49753	51692	962
7	leadership qualities	46170	7310	6316
8	transformational leadership	37522	10284	3648
9	amazon leadership principles	35939	6842	5252
10	what is leadership	28604	8706	3285
11	types of leadership	27897	12045	2316
12	leadership training	25908	48715	531
13	leadership books	24200	4220	5734
14	leadership skills	23976	3983	6019
15	thought leadership	21653	29328	738
16	international leadership of texas	20040	4031	4971
17	leadership questions	19885	52340	379
18	different types of leadership	18612	4338	4290
19	democratic leadership	18198	16182	1124
20	women in leadership	18071	7169	2520

This image is of an Excel spreadsheet. The sheet has keyword data for the search "leadership." It is sorted by demand from largest to smallest. That shows us the keywords people are searching for most often, in descending order. An author of this hypothetical book would want to have "leadership" in the title or subtitle. That keyword is so competitive and the category so broad. There are more than 60,000 books on leadership on Amazon at the moment.

For these reasons, the author would probably want to narrow it down somewhat. Perhaps the book will be *Leadership Quotes* or *Leadership Styles*.

Look at the cell that is selected. You'll see that "Amazon leadership principles" has nearly 36,000 searches a month. "Leadership books" is searched for nearly 24,000 times a month. Clearly, people are searching for books in this genre.

Based on the information in this chart alone, our author might use the following in the outline:

- What is leadership
- Leadership quotes
- Servant leadership
- Leadership definition
- Leadership styles
- Leadership training
- Leadership skills
- Thought leadership
- Women in leadership

In the outline or Table of Contents, it might look like this:

Title: What is Leadership?

Chapter 1: Leadership definition

Chapter 2: Leadership styles (include servant leadership here)

Chapter 3: Leadership training

Chapter 4: Leadership skills

Chapter 5: Women in leadership

Chapter 6: Thought leadership

Chapter 7: Leadership quotes

With most books having about 10 chapters, this one search alone put our author 70% of the way to outlining the book. A look at Publisher Rocket, and the outline is complete.

To outline your book now and position it well on Amazon later, buy KWR tools. The one that goes with a membership at Site Build It is great, and so is Publisher Rocket. Use them.

Begin the draft of your book outline.

Book Outlining Workshop: Let SEO outline your book for you

How to outline a book is something that stumps many authors. They have a general idea of what they want to go into their book. They don't know all of the details and aren't certain of what should go into it and what should be left out.

Every client I've done this for has loved it. I take into account what the author wants to do, the intended audience, and other factors. Then, I go straight for the KWR. You can find out more about KWR, outlining, and more at HarshmanServices.com

Literature Review

A literature review is simply looking at what currently is in print related to your topic.

Amazon is the best place to do this. Either use Publisher Rocket, or open an incognito window in your internet browser. This keeps Amazon's knowledge of your previous searches from affecting your search results.

Go to Amazon within that incognito window, and look at 10–15 books that are like yours. Use the Look Inside feature on all of them that have it available. Read each Table of Contents, and see what those books have there.

Most likely, you'll find that there's quite a bit of overlap—that about 50% to 75% of the content is the same across those books. You'll probably want to be sure your book covers all of that overlapping content, too.

Here's where it gets fun. You might find some things you didn't think of yet. Then you get to decide whether to include those things in your book.

If you look carefully and think about it, you will also identify some content gaps. Those are areas not covered by those books. Were those things left out because they shouldn't be covered? Or have you identified an area of opportunity?

What if it's an opportunity to provide something readers could use? Put it in your outline.

Options for DIY and DFY

If you don't like the traditional Roman Numeral One method but want more help, try my Mind Mapping Workshop.

If you want to know exactly what to put in your book and where, you'll love the Let SEO Outline Your Book for You workshop.

Readers of this book can get their outline done for 50% off.

Go to https://hs.ck.page/products/write-my-outline and make your payment, then we'll contact you about your specific needs, and we'll do the rest!

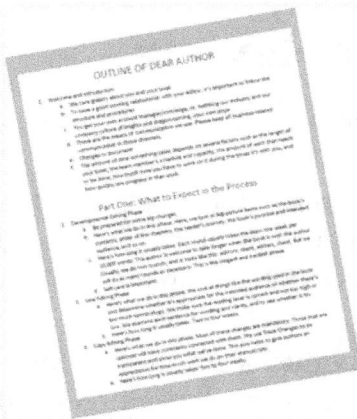

$199.00

Write My Outline for Me!

We access, analyze, and apply research that allows us to create your nonfiction book's outline for you. Other authors agonize for days and weeks over their outline, but you're smarter than that!

Get it now!

Outlining Service

We include this in the writing program called Your Book Bakery: 12 Weeks to a Manuscript.

The only purpose of your outline is to help you stay focused by telling you what goes where. It tells your editors the same. The outline does not have to be in full sentences. Neither must it be parallel or pretty. This is just a tool that won't be seen by your readers—for now. It will morph into your Table of Contents later. For now, just put together something that works for this stage.

Be sure that your outline follows a logical path, taking the reader from Point A to Pont B in a way that makes sense.

Make your outline thorough. Then, when you sit down to write a portion of your book, you will know exactly what needs to go in that section. This makes writing your book so much easier.

Other Planning

Aside from your outline—the chapters and other main content of your book—you'll need to plan things like these:

- Pull quotes (aka callout boxes)—do you want to use them and if so, what do you want them to look like? For this book, I knew very early on that I wanted to have callouts and action items. Also, the pull quotes had to be on baked goods instead of the usual rectangles. The action items needed a whisk as a symbol of doing something.

- Interviews—who would you like to talk to about your book?
- Quotations—which books or other sources do you want to use portions of? Which do you need to secure permissions for?
- Which resources do you want to recommend to your readers?
- Do you want to have quizzes, charts, lines for writing?
- Will you need to have pages created on your website before your book is published?
- Podcast tours and other promotion
- Beta readers
- Foreword—whom will you ask to write it?
- Endorsements—whom will you ask to say good things about your book?
- Blog posts
- Social media posts
- Videos such as a book trailer
- Dedication
- Acknowledgments—keep a list of people who have helped you along the way.
- Maps or other original drawings or illustrations
- Editing—schedule your editors months ahead of time.
- Cover designer (We have a valuable form for you in the Resources section.)
- Formatting
- Do you need a book marketer, or will you handle all of that yourself?
- Will you have a workbook or companion journal for your book?
- PDFs and other lead magnets you'll put on your website that relate to your book

Whisk Together

Buy and use the suggested keyword research tools.

- Publisher Rocket https://harshman6776--rocket.thrivecart. com/publisher-rocket/
- Solo Build It! is http://www.sitesell.com/Jennifer360.html
- Solo Build II! for WP is http://sbiwp.sitesell.com/ Jennifer360.html

Download and print mind map sheets to use. https://www. harshmanservices.com/free-mind-map-starter-sheet/

Mind map your book.

Start here with a possible topic or title.

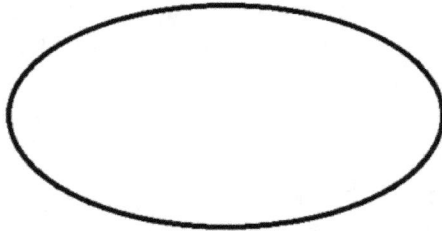

My Book Title

Chapter 8: Tips for Beginning Authors

Here are some tips I give beginning authors.

- To be good at anything, you may have to be bad at it first.
- Write simply.
- Dump the words on the page as fast as you can.
- Follow your outline, but you don't have to write the chapters in order.
- Use a timer and race it.
- Use rituals, totems, and anything else that works for you. Your brain will make the association if you're consistent.
- Sneak in two minutes here and there throughout the day, every day you can. Be nice to yourself even when you can't.
- Try recording yourself. Listen to it later, jotting the good stuff. It won't all be good. Everyone rambles, and that's okay.

Crumbling Writer's Block

How many times have people asked me how to get over writer's block? Approximately once for every granule of sugar in a bakery.

You get over writer's block in any of a hundred (or more) ways. Here are a few just to get you started.

- Use a creativity guide like *A Whack on the Side of the Head* or *A Kick in the Seat of the Pants*, both books by Roger von Oech. Things like that have idea-generating exercises. For example, they have you select a few words at random and use them as a writing prompt.

- If you have the board game Taboo, get it out. Pull a card and get started. Write about the word or phrase at the top of the card without using the forbidden words at the bottom of the card.
- Write the worst sentence you can think of. You read that right. Write an awful sentence, and just keep going. As long as you don't *leave* in your manuscript anything that's horrible when you're done, it'll be fine.
- Make a list of all of the *other* things that your mind wants to write, or things that are bugging you. Just dump it all out on the page. Then just keep writing. You may find a gem.

With all of these, the idea is to get something on your paper (or screen). Something, anything. You can delete it or rework it later.

Another approach is to set it aside and do something else. Go for a walk. Take a nap. Make a healthful snack. Visit with a friend. Read a book. Think of those times when you're trying hard to remember something, but you can't. You finally give up and go grab a cookie. Right in the middle of the third bite of that delicious diversion, *bam*, the thing you gave up on trying to remember comes up out of your memory like the batter in a popover. You drop your snack (poor cookie) and run. Setting aside the piece you're writing — for a little while — is like that. You'll be in the middle of something else (sleeping, showering), and the idea will pop up out of the depths. Get thee to the keyboard, and capture the ideas that have come.

Turn off your inner editor. This is a habit you have to build, and it's hard! Set a timer for two minutes. Then type as fast as you can, telling yourself you will fix it later. I call this impersonating Kermit the Frog on the keyboard.

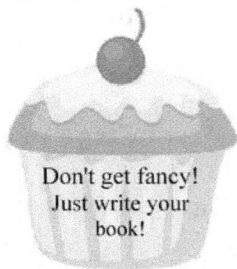

Don't get fancy! Just write your book!

Decorating Too Soon

Many authors want to make their Microsoft Word document look like a book. That's understandable. They *are* writing a book, after all. They want to see what it might look like when it's finished. Some people find it motivating. The pages sure do fill up quickly when the margins are set to 6x9 inches. It's problematic, though, and should not be done.

Don't get fancy. What are some examples of things authors might do when they start getting fancy and decorating too soon?

Multiple fonts

When getting fancy, authors tend to use several different fonts for the body and headings. Authors want the headings to be in a different font from the body text. They will be different when the book is finished. That's not needed yet.

There are two options for headings. The first is to type them in the regular font and next to them, put the level of heading they should be:

Decorating Too Soon [H2].

The other option is to use the Ribbon in MS Word to set your headings. Keep the headings consistent with the hierarchy in your outline.

- Chapter titles can be Heading 1 (H1).
- Big divisions within chapters can all be Heading 2 (H2).
- Subheadings are Heading 3 (H3).
- If sections that have H3 on them need to be divided further, use Heading 4 (H4).

It's not common for a book to need Heading 5 or beyond, but it can happen. If you find yourself in that territory, reconsider the complexity of your outline. Try to limit the number of sections that need that many heading levels.

Inserting glyphs and images

Some authors get fancy by inserting glyphs to separate sections of writing. Glyphs are symbols. In many books, three spaced asterisks * * * serve the purpose.

Glyphs can be used in a nonfiction book, especially if certain symbols lend themselves to your topic. It can be an important part of your book's branding.

Some of the books I've edited are in the Lead Like a Pirate series. They have icons such as a compass and a bomb to draw the readers' attention to certain things.

Better Leaders Better Schools Roadmap is a book I developed. In it, an image of a pencil lies across the cover and the top of certain pages. The section headings and chapter titles are printed on the pencil.

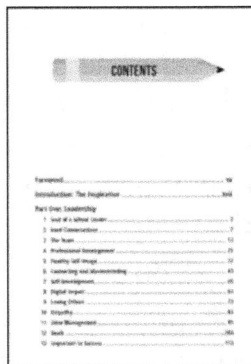

The glyphs in these books were not added until the formatting stage. That was long after the writing stage.

If you have some ideas for things you might want to include, make note of them somewhere. Your repository is a great place to keep everything. Wait until the right time to do anything with the ideas.

Chances are high that authors will add images that they don't realize are the wrong size or resolution. Those images might look good in the Microsoft Word document. They will look pixilated or blurry in the book.

Changing margins

Microsoft Word's default page size is 8.5x11 inches. Many authors change the margins or paper size to make it look like a book page. It seems harmless enough, and that is a way for an author to see major progress as they write. The page count racks up fast when the margins are set to 6x9 inches rather than full-size sheets.

The margins and page size must be changed back before the manuscript goes to editing. No editor wants to work in a strange and unwieldy format. The settings certainly need to be reset before it goes to layout. Some formatters will charge extra if they have to undo your formatting, so please keep this in mind. It's fine if you want to boost your morale and motivation by changing your MS Word document's page size. Change it back before you send it to anyone.

In doing things like this, authors waste not only their own time but their editor or agency's time, too. All of that has to be stripped out and redone. It's best to just mix your batter at this stage.

Using text boxes

These are the bane of many a formatter's existence. At Harshman Services, our editors go above and beyond, so they do some of the formatter's tasks. If there are text boxes present, we strip them out. This benefits our clients even if they go to someone else for the next phase and use us only for the editing. Because we instruct our clients never to use text boxes, if we have to strip out text boxes, there is an extra charge for that.

Being Determined and Committed

When you sit down to write, no one and nothing else exists until you come up for air. That might be an hour or 2,000 words later. Yes, it is possible to write more than 2,000 words in an hour (as long as you can type at least 34 words per minute). Start with a much smaller number of words or a much shorter time. Build up to it. I usually tell my students to start with two minutes.

Before you sit down, clear the decks. Have a clean work surface. Sweep it into a bread basket if you need to.

Silence your phone and anything else that could distract you. Use apps that block social media and other websites if you need that (see Resources). There is no shame in this.

Donald Roos wrote *Don't Read This Book: Time Management for Creative People*. In it, he said, "If you work on too many ideas at once, you run the risk of all your ideas constantly being half finished." Around here, we'd call them half baked. I have half-baked manuscripts on my hard drive.

Avoid that trap.

Go to the bathroom and grab a drink before you sit down to write.

Then turn off the spelling and grammar checker on your word processing program. I'm serious about removing anything that might distract you.

Bang those keys (or scratch the pen across the paper). Enjoy every minute carefree as you morsha borsha bake a cake-a. No deleting, no overthinking, and no editing! Dump words on the page!

Whisk Together

Write a couple of tips you'll keep in mind.

_____

_____

_____

Write your get-ready-to-write routine here.

_____

_____

_____

_____

_____

_____

Chapter 9: Writing Your Book (& What's Next)

Your Research

For this book, you should write what you already know, not something you'll need to do extensive research on. You'll still need to look up a few things, perhaps conduct a few interviews via email or phone (HARO to the rescue). But the research shouldn't take you more than a couple of days total. Research. Take notes, and especially keep a record of any and every resource you use. If something is not common knowledge, you must cite the source.

You might want to use Scrivener or Evernote. You can also go old-school and use index cards or a physical notebook. Make it easy on yourself whenever you can. There's no award for who worked the hardest on their book. If it's easier, take screenshots instead of typing or writing out notes. Screenshots count! As long as you can see the url or other source name, you can type it up for your citations. Who cares if you didn't take the time to write it by hand!

Interview anyone you need to for your book, and record the interviews. Transcribe them (there are some free tools for this). It might create a large portion of content for your book. You can also use these as freebies, lead magnets, or other bonus content.

It may be tempting to think that in previous years, you've done all the research you need to do for this book. Please put the time and effort into it anyway.

You already know most of what you need to know to write this particular book. But almost every book involves some research, even if it's making sure your information is still up to date.

How you go about it is up to you. You may choose between researching in order of your chapters, or topically:

- the people in the book on one day
- the locations on another
- the events, statistics, etc.

Pick the approach that appeals to you most.

Your Book's Structure

Different cakes have different structures. On the left is a simple one-layer sheet cake for a retirement party.

On the right is a four-tier wedding cake, complicated and impressive. Between the two, there are many variations.

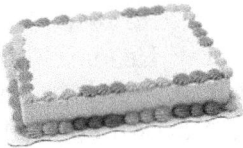

Books can have different structures, too. Here are some of the tried-and-true book structures.

1. List

The list is a straightforward and familiar structure. It's great for books that have a series of similar or related items, such as principles or lessons. Books that use it often offer simple solutions to complex problems. Books with numbers in the title are often using this structure.

2. One, Two, Three

This format is for books that offer a new interpretation of a familiar idea or a new set of solutions for a problem. Chapters are grouped into parts that come in a logical order. Part One is called "the why." It describes the problem you intend to solve. Then it tells why it's bad, explains its causes, or gives other foundational information. Part Two is "the what" section and contains your solution. It often constitutes the main portion of the book in both volume and impact. Part Three is a big serving of "the how." It explains how the reader should apply your method or system.

3. Ideas and Exercises

The first half of the book posits your theory, and the second instructs the reader to do exercises. This may be a coaching book, or it could contain recipes or project instructions. A book on having a dog might open with an overview of breeds and basic information. Then it might dig into training techniques. If you want your readers to embrace your philosophy and take action, you might want to use this structure.

4. The Essay/Thought Leadership Book

This is for a customized process that can't really be broken into steps or has steps that overlap. It's also a good structure for setting forth new thinking (thought leadership).

5. Bits and Pieces

These books have a variety of loosely related parts that don't need to go in any particular order.

6. Parable/Memoir

This is telling a story that has a lesson or is true. The hard part is doing it in a way that people will want to read it. A parable should focus on a single lesson. A memoir should focus on a single "chapter" of the subject's life, not entire life.

There are two main approaches: story and message. The first must be engaging. The second must be clear. Either way, make sure the narrative stays on track. Memoirs are hard to do well, and they are even harder to market and sell. If you're famous, have a stunning story, or intend to market your book as a full-time job, this format can be very effective for you.

Your Chapter Structure

First, we should address the elephant ear in the room: what is a chapter, and how long should it be? A chapter is a section or division of a book. Each chapter has a number or title (or both). Each chapter is related to the overall theme or topic of the book.

With children's picture books being the exception, almost all books have chapters.

Purpose of chapters

The main purpose of a chapter is to break up the material. Most readers need breaks while reading a book. They feel guilty for stopping in the middle of a section. Chapter divisions give them the rest they need. If you don't give it to them, they'll likely put down your book and never pick it up again.

Chapters can be divided by chronology, topic, or impact, for example.

It might be tempting to think of chapters as nothing more than dividing lines in a book. That is akin to thinking that sugar goes into the batter only to change the taste. It would be a big mistake, so we're not going to do that.

Chapters are an essential element that affect the quality of your book. They pace the content, focus a reader's attention where you want it, and give the reader a rest at the end of each chapter. Think chapter break = reader's break.

Each chapter should have a clear purpose. That should be planned during the outlining phase. Each one has a topic that fits within the book's theme and contributes to the overall statement of your book.

Theses

Your book should have a central statement or thesis. You discovered or determined it during the foundational questions. Look at the spot that says, "Describe your book in one sentence." Now make it an assertion or statement your book will make to a reader." That assertion is your book's thesis statement. **Write it on the lines provided.**

Every chapter needs a thesis, too. You don't necessarily have to start your chapter with it or even include it at all, although you can. Feel free to think of it as a one-sentence description just for you of what that chapter is about.

It could look like this:

Chapter one is about the questions every new author has about writing a book.

Chapter two is about accepting that you must write a book.

Chapter three is an overview of the entire process to prepare the new author for the process of baking a book.

These chapters each have their own thesis. All support the larger statement: anyone can bake a book if they have the right ingredients.

How long a chapter should be

The chapters should be roughly the same length. It's okay if most chapters have 2,000 words and one has 4,000. Suppose you have several 2,000-word chapters and one 12,000-word chapter. Your book might appear lopsided. Consider cutting the big chapter into pieces.

Keep track of word count as you're writing. The industry standard for a page is 250 words. If you've drafted a chapter that is 10,000 words long, it will take up 40 pages in the final book. That is an eternity between breaks for the reader. Also, most books have about 10 chapters. If they're all about the same length . . . Ring that up on the register, and you'll see that the book would be massive. We're not baking a 12-tier wedding cake here.

That's a huge job for everyone involved:

- for you to write and revise
- for your editors to edit
- for your formatter to lay out
- for your reader to read

How can you cut that down to size? Perhaps you create the basic batter for your book. Then whip up some of the content on your website. Bake some into your subscriber emails. Sprinkle some into podcast episodes or mini books you sell on Amazon.

Basic elements of chapter structure

Keep in mind that there are many variations possible. Here are the basic elements of chapter structure.

- A title or headline
- An introduction that grabs the reader's interest
- Body paragraphs that provide information
- A recap or summary of the chapter
- A transition to the next chapter

There are several options for each structure. What you'll choose will depend on your book's purpose and your personal preference. Some authors use epigraphs at the beginning of chapters; some don't. Some use a story or example at the beginning of a chapter. Then they have the explanation or exposition in the middle and action steps at the end. One might also include lines for writing. The reader can answer questions the author posed or take notes right there in the book.

Now let's look at a few of the various structures.

Various chapter structures

3B Chapter Structure: Benefit, Barrier, Belief

It takes this form. How to (insert the benefit here) without having to (pose the barrier here) even if (state the belief here). The chapter title could be exactly that phrasing.

Demonstrate a benefit. What's the benefit of this chapter? What insight will your readers gain?

Show a barrier. What barriers or obstacles are your readers facing? What is their problem? What do your readers currently believe right now?

Reveal a belief. What belief(s) or inner thoughts are your readers telling themselves about your topic? Help them beat it.

3E Chapter Structure: Expositing, Equipping, Engaging

Here is a very effective chapter structure. It's what I call the 3E Structure: Expositing, Equipping, Engaging. When authors use the 3E Structure, they tell a story or explain something, give useful information, then direct the reader to take action. As you can see in the examples below, which both use the 3E Structure, the same recipe can be used quite differently by different people.

You can see the 3E Structure used in my client Susie Tomenchok's book *The Art of Everyday Negotiation without Manipulation*. First is the beginning of the chapter.

Chapter 1—Negotiation Has a Bad Reputation

Get comfortable, lean in, and label yourself a negotiator.

Mark and Gary were both senior vice presidents at the same Fortune 50 company, although they were in different divisions.

Gary's team managed the huge technical facility along with all of the office space. Gary held the largest office, which was located on the second floor in the corner. It was quite large with a space for a couch and a conference table. Two walls with full-length windows overlooked the mountains. His position warranted the office because hundreds of people within his organization were also officed in the building, and he often held meetings all day long.

Mark's office was located on the opposite corner of the building. While also a corner office, it was not as nice of a view since it overlooked an empty lot adjacent to the parking. It was still one of the largest offices in the building. Mark's opinion was that since he and Gary were on the same level in the organizational chart, his office should be exactly the same size as Gary's office.

So, he went to Gary's office after hours and counted his ceiling

As you can see, it starts with a story. This captures the reader's attention and sets the stage for what's to come. Humans love stories. It's in our nature, and there are some helpful books on this topic, which you'll find on my website.

Then the chapter contains information for the reader.

This isn't everything from that chapter, just part of it. That chapter ends with this:

There is an Ask Yourself section and a Take Action section. By including these, Tomenchok engages her readers and helps them move along the path of transformation she wants them to walk. Negotiating is becoming easier for them, and that is her book's goal.

38 • Susie Tomenchok

🧠 Ask Yourself

- How do I look at negotiation?
- How many times have I negotiated in life?
- Why does negotiation bring any negative emotion?
- Do I want to be an advocate for my situations?

Take Action

- Have awareness now in every conversation you attend. Seeing it as a negotiation means you are considering all of the various angles—for yourself as well as the other side.
- Guide the other person to see and understand your story and how an agreement will help them as well.
- Watch your emotion and the emotion of the other person. Keep shifting to retain or gain objectivity.
- Explore approaches where everyone continues to be neutral.
- Work on getting to closing. Formalize decisions and include next steps. Have the other side reiterate the agreements.

4D Chapter Structure: Define, Describe, Depict, Direct

Another variation is the 4D structure:

Define. (What is it?)
Describe. (What does it look like?)
Depict. (Can you give us examples?)
Direct. (What are the action steps?)

TAC Chapter Structure

Topic
Argument
Conclusion

TRACE Chapter Structure

Topic: Present the topic, issue, or question the chapter addresses.

Rules: Share the rules, situation, or lay of the land.

Application: Show how the reader can apply the information.

Conclusion: State what the outcome would be.

Engagement: Give the reader action steps to take.

Note that when the TRACE method is used, sometimes one or more of the letters will be left out. The letters will not always be applied in the order given here.

Other chapter structures

There are also chapter structures that don't have any fancy names. Here are some examples:

- Storytelling or narrative
- Chronology or in order
- How-to or step-by-step

Some books have certain elements within the chapters, such as a section of questions to ponder or actions to take. *School of Grit* by Brad Ritter has Pack Your Rucksack and another section called Challenge, for example. Dan Miller's *48 Days to the Work and Life You Love*, another book I edited, has a section titled Countdown to Work I Love.

Which structure you choose and whether you insert elements like those will depend on what you want your book to be like.

Give this some thought. Pick. Then stick with it.

Seeing if Previous Content Fits

Repurposing content is turning one thing into something (or several somethings) else. Your podcast can become your blog posts, which can become your book. My mentor, friend, and client John Stange makes what he calls a content waterfall. He uses it to create multiple podcasts, posts for his massive blog that Google loves, books, and more.

When you look through your files, you will probably find things you've already written. Maybe they're incomplete, mere snippets here and there. That's okay. If some of it fits, and I am emphasizing *if it fits*, use it. If it does not fit, that's okay, too. You'll probably be able to use it in another book.

Work Routine and Rituals

Do the following daily until your first draft is complete:

- Perform your get-to-work routine and rituals.
- Write until your day's word count/time limit is reached.
- Participate in self-care, and reward yourself for a day well done.

That night, do *The Almost-Magic Notebook* and create the next day's to-do list from that night's entry. Knowing what you're going to be writing about tomorrow gives your brain a head start because it will be working on it while you sleep.

Writing Your Book

Begin writing your first draft. The key is to turn off your inner editor while you write. It is quite a trick, but you can do it. Try starting with a timer set for two minutes. Bang the keys as fast as you can, telling yourself, "I can fix it after the timer beeps." After you've gone for two minutes, it's okay to stop and clean up what you wrote. If you can keep going for a while, do that.

After you can go for two minutes, go for three. Then five. Then ten. Before you know it, you'll be like Kermit the Frog on his typewriter. Words will fill up your pages faster than you can imagine when you first start the practice.

During this stage, just dump the words on the page as fast as you can. While it's great if you have complete sentences, it's okay to have some phrases here and there. You can come back later and complete them.

When you are drafting your book, you can start with what you know and write about it. You can add to what you know, and write about that. You can start writing about something you don't know, learn what you need to know to fill in the gaps, then write that part.

When I wrote articles, I didn't want anything to slow me down. I could write the bulk of an article (about 90% of each piece) without knowing statistics or dates. I would write and then go find the missing data and fill in the gaps.

When you come to a spot in your writing where you don't know the name, date, or stat, type two asterisks (**). Keep going. It looks like this: Here's the beginning of the sentence that's missing a fact or a date ** and here's the end of the sentence. You can also put into brackets a note to yourself about what you need to do there [I need to explain this phenomenon in more detail]. By the time your book is finished, all of those bracketed notes to self will be deleted.

No more deleting

Forget the Backspace key. You will clean it up, but *not while you're drafting*.

If you must remove something from your writing, just cut and paste it into another document. Call that document Spare Parts, Parking Lot, or Idea Cellar, or, as we call it, your Idea Pantry. You never know how, where, or when that snippet of writing might come in handy.

I have seen entire books spring from a paragraph and even from one sentence that was cut (not deleted, cut) from a manuscript because it did not fit that book. This could only happen because the author put it into an Idea Pantry.

Because of this, you will never again delete something you've written, okay? Every time you sit down to revise your writing, open your Idea Pantry first. Paste into your Idea Pantry anything you cut from your manuscript.

When you get stuck, ask yourself a question to get the words flowing again. You could also use a tool such as Article Forge (https://www.articleforge.com/?ref=c9c7d0) to help you generate some words. There is no shame in using tools to help you be more effective.

If you hate writing

Do you remember that at the beginning of this book, I said you don't have to write your book to write your book? I said I would explain later. Well, it's later. There are two main options for you if you hate writing.

You can hire a ghostwriter. A ghostwriter will talk to you and turn those interviews into a book for you. I have some friends and colleagues who are highly skilled ghostwriters. See the Resources section for the Ghostwriter Directory.

You can record yourself talking. Transcribe the audio files manually or using an AI tool. Then you turn that (or have an editor turn that) material into a book.

Consistency

While you're writing the first draft of your book, it's great if you can write every day, even for just a few minutes. Maybe you can't manage that with your schedule. Or you're a batcher like I am (I dumped more than 13,000 words into this manuscript the first day). If so, then write on the days you can. Work hard to stay on schedule. I didn't write every day on this book, but I made up for it by writing 4,000 words per day on the days I did write. Don't think you have to do that! Books bake in my brain for years before I sit down to write them. Once I do, it's like pressing the nozzle on a can of whipped cream and holding it until all the product is out of the can.

During your daily writing time, it's okay to set a timer and use the Pomodoro Technique. Play "race the clock." Take short breaks if you need to. Five minutes with your eyes closed and listening to soothing music can do amazing things.

Done is better than perfect. Say it with me. Done is better than perfect. You will level the cake (revise it) later. You will frost it (format it and put the finishing touches on it) even later than that. For now, just get your first draft written. If you need any help doing that, feel free to reach out to me via email: Jennifer@ HarshmanServices.com. To sign up for a session of Your Book Bakery: 12 Weeks to a Manuscript, go to www.harshmanservices. com/your-book-bakery

When you are finished writing your first draft, put it away and do something else for a month. Perhaps you go on a podcast tour about the book you're writing. Or you could start posting parts of it as blog posts. You could also pick up a new skill. Give the book time to rest just as you would bread dough after it's been worked for a while.

After that time has passed, read through it with a proverbial red pen in hand. Make notes to yourself. Which parts are unclear? Which ones need more material because it seems like you glossed over things? Where did you get too wordy?

After you revise it on your own, seek help from a developmental editor. We have a few of each type of editor at my agency.

Keep in mind that you can do this. All you need is the right mindset and recipe to follow. I've given you one. Do you have the other? If not, join me for some coaching. If so, then go, go, go!

Ready, set, go!

The Recipe

Below, you'll find a recipe that walks you through the process of writing your book. If you follow it, you'll have your first draft written in a few weeks and ready to hand to an editor in a few months. Note that for the sake of saving space, some of the items will instruct you to refer to previous sections of this book.

You are welcome to use all of this on your own. You're also welcome to apply to join the program Your Book Bakery so you'll have ongoing support and a special prize for writing your book. Earn a reward for sending people to it. For each person who joins because of you, you'll receive a referral bonus of $100.

The program goes beyond what this book can do. It walks you through a proven recipe for writing a nonfiction book in 12 weeks. We give a list of the ingredients needed, show you how to put it all together, and help you bake it so it comes out just right. It's only fair to warn you that doing it in 12 weeks is usually intense and takes a lot out of participants. That's why I suggest self-care throughout. But it's all worth it.

This book does not cover the process of publishing or of marketing your book. Those are akin to decorating and displaying your baked good (your book). My other books can help you with those parts, but it's separate from this. While it is best to work with Harshman Services all the way through the writing and publishing process, you *can* do it yourself. You can also come to us when you get stuck.

Whisk Together

This chapter has a long list of action steps. It has 12 weeks' worth of them, in fact. Read the manual and check out the resources.

The Program

Below, you'll find the 12-week program for writing the first draft of a book. Not everyone wants to write one that quickly, and that's okay. Set the schedule you prefer.

Please do these things in order. One day per week is allowed for a Sabbath or other rest, for those who decide to take it. You don't have to. If you're the type of person who gets off track if they take a break, please keep going instead of taking that day off. You may journal Scripture or do some other spiritual writing. Maintain your momentum. Check in with your accountability partner every day, even if you're taking the day off.

Week One

Recommended Resources:

Project Management for Writers by Terry Stafford

Site Build It! (For their keyword tool)

☐ Begin setting up your business legally if you haven't already. Follow your state and local laws. This process may take several weeks and won't be mentioned in this book again, so do what you need to do when it is time. When I did it, it took three weeks of running a DBA ad in the local paper before I could apply for my business license. Then the county clerk granted me the license the day that was complete.

☐ Be realistic about what you can do during these 12 weeks. This means acknowledge that you have work/family obligations, so you can't just write for 16 hours a day. It also means clearing off your counters so you can bake this book. Get rid of or pause any commitments that are not life-and-death issues. I promise, everyone but tiny humans who depend on you for sustenance can make it without you for a while. Your spouse can shop and cook. Your children won't die if you don't help them with school or chauffer them around. The nonprofits will find someone to handle all the things. In 12 weeks from now, you can choose whether to pick up any of those commitments again.

☐ Set your schedule for this project if you haven't already. Decide on a time of day that you'll write and for how long. Filling out an intention statement and setting up a commitment device will help you. Set a backup time in case life interferes (it has a way of doing that), so that you will be able to keep your commitment. Do you have trouble getting things done? Be sure to work with your accountability partner. Get on the writing sprint sessions we host on Zoom. There is at least one session per weekday, and you may ask for other times if the scheduled slot doesn't work for you.

☐ Schedule time for contacting people daily, because you'll be doing at least three per day for the next 90 days.

☐ Create your writing environment. This includes the physical (building, room, desk, computer) and the mental (music or quiet, working alone or with people, etc.). Choose one device and one software program to use for writing. If you prefer drafting with pen and paper, that's fine, as long as you enter each day's words into your computer. I recommend using Microsoft Word, but the tool doesn't matter nearly as much as using it consistently does. The right tool is the one you will use. Have a way to capture the ideas that come to you when you're doing something else. Recording yourself talking into your phone is fine. You can talk your book instead of writing it. Again, do whatever works for you.

- ☐ Be determined. When you sit down to write, no one and nothing else exists until you come up for air. That might be 1 hour or 2,000 words later, whichever is greater. Yes, it is possible to write more than 2,000 words in an hour (as long as you can type at least 34 words per minute). Before you sit down, clear the decks, silence your phone and anything else that you could be distracted by. Go to the bathroom first. Then, when you set your timer or otherwise get started, bang those keys like a madman. No deleting, no overthinking, and *no editing*. Dump words on the page!

- ☐ Create a folder or other repository where you'll collect everything related to your book. Some people like to use Evernote or Google Drive for this. Start putting everything that relates to your book in there.

- ☐ Choose an audience you want to serve and a problem you want to help them solve. Look at your answers to the questions in chapter two.

- ☐ Describe in three sentences the book you want to write.

- ☐ Describe your book in one sentence. Now make it an assertion or statement your book will make to your reader.

- ☐ Define your goals.

- ☐ Buy access to KWR tools. Use them, or ask Jennifer for help.

- ☐ Analyze the KWR you conducted, and let SEO outline your book for you. Watch my recorded workshop if desired and ask for clarification if you need it. Begin the draft of your book outline.

- ☐ Be sure that your outline follows a logical path, taking the reader from Point A to Pont B in a way that makes sense.

- ☐ Be sure that your outline is thorough. You want it to be so complete that when you sit down to write a portion of your book, you will know exactly what needs to go in that section. Finish the draft of your book outline. Share it with someone you trust for feedback. Detach yourself emotionally from whenever you get feedback on anything you've created. Thank everyone for the feedback, no matter what. Remember they are trying to help you make your book the best it can be.

☐ Decide which format your book will take. Think about the structure you want your book to have. Consider the relationship between the chapters and how to organize them to create a better reading experience. Select an organizing principle that makes it easier for readers to digest your information and keeps them turning pages. Remember the common types:

    1. List

    2. One, Two, Three

    3. Ideas and Exercises

    4. The Essay/Thought Leadership Book

    5. Bits & Pieces

    6. Parable/Memoir

☐ Choose three self-care actions you'll take on a regular basis.

☐ Choose three rewards you'll give yourself: small, medium, and large.

☐ Cheer yourself and others on because you're doing something wonderful, and it's going to change the world.

☐ Jot down notes regarding everything in Week One, put it all into your folder/repository, and make all the decisions you need to make. If you finish all of this before the week is over, move on to Week Two, and start doing the small amount of research you'll need to do for this book.

Your Progress

You should know what you're baking, what needs to go into it, and how the recipe reads.

Week Two

You shouldn't need to do much research for this book, but there's probably a little that you need to do. Take notes, and especially keep a record of any and every resource you use. If something is not common knowledge, you must cite the source.

You might want to use Scrivener or Evernote for this. You can also go old-school and use index cards or a physical notebook. Make it easy on yourself whenever you can. There's no award for who worked the hardest on their book. If it's easier, take screenshots instead of typing or writing out notes. Screenshots count! As long as you can see the url or other source name so you can type it up for your citations, who cares if you didn't take the time to write it by hand!

Interview anyone you need to for your book, and record the interviews. Transcribe them (there are some free tools for this), and you might create a substantial amount of content for your book. You can also use these as freebies, lead magnets, or other bonus content.

Start a style sheet for your book. See the enclosed example. If you have any questions, just ask on the call.

Make note of any of your struggles you are aware of when it comes to writing. Do you tend to overuse a certain word/phrase? Do you use overly long sentences? These will be things to keep in mind as you write and to let your editor (and beta readers and fellow Book Bakers) know. They can help you with them.

You already know most of what you need to know to write this particular book. But almost every book involves some research, even if it's making sure your information is up to date.

How you go about it is up to you. You may research in order of your chapters or topically. Pick the approach that appeals to you more.

Day one of week two

- ☐ Research anything needed for chapter one and six.
- ☐ Do one self-care activity.

- ☐ Treat yourself with one small reward.
- ☐ Check in with your accountability partner.

Day two of week two

- ☐ Research anything needed for chapter two and seven.
- ☐ Do one self-care activity.
- ☐ Treat yourself with one small reward.
- ☐ Check in with your accountability partner.

Day three of week two

- ☐ Research anything needed for chapter three and eight.
- ☐ Do one self-care activity.
- ☐ Treat yourself with one small reward.
- ☐ Check in with your accountability partner.

Day four of week two

- ☐ Research anything needed for chapter four and nine.
- ☐ Do one self-care activity.
- ☐ Treat yourself with one small reward.
- ☐ Check in with your accountability partner.
- ☐ Do one self-care activity, and treat yourself with one small reward.
- ☐ Check in with your accountability partner.

Day five of week two

- ☐ Research anything needed for chapter five and ten.
- ☐ Do one self-care activity.
- ☐ Treat yourself with one small reward.
- ☐ Check in with your accountability partner.

Day six of week two

If you have more than ten chapters, research anything needed for the remaining chapters.

- ☐ Make a list of the people you'd like to endorse your book.
- ☐ Do one self-care activity.
- ☐ Treat yourself with this week's medium-sized reward.

☐ Check in with your accountability partner.

Day seven of week two

☐ Take the day off, or keep going. Either way, check in with your accountability partner, and do self-care.

Your Progress

You should have your research done now. The oven is preheating.

Week Three

This is when you begin writing your first draft. During this stage, just dump the words on the page as fast as you can. While it's great if you have complete sentences, it's okay to have some phrases here and there. You can come back later and complete them.

When you get to something you don't know, need to find, etc., remember to type two asterisks where the missing material belongs. You can also type notes to yourself in brackets.

Forget the Backspace key. If you must remove something from your writing, just cut and paste it into another document. Call that document your Idea Pantry (or whatever you'd like). You will never again delete something you've written, okay? You never know how, where, or when it might come in handy.

When you get stuck, ask yourself a question to get the words flowing again. You could also use a tool such as Article Forge to help you generate some words.

It's okay to set a timer and use the Pomodoro Technique. Play "race the clock." Take short breaks if you need to. Five minutes with your eyes closed and listening to soothing music can do amazing things.

Schedule any interviews you weren't able to conduct last week.

Day one of week three

☐ Make a copy of your outline.

☐ Pick a section to write (whatever seems tasty to you that day).

☐ Turn off your internal editor/judge, and dump the words on the page as quickly as you can. Go for one hour or produce 2,000 words, whichever is greater.

☐ Enter your word count in the word count tracker.

□   Do one self-care activity.

□   Treat yourself with one small reward.

□   Check in with your accountability partner.

Day two of week three

□   Write for one hour or produce 2,000 words.

□   Enter your word count in the word count tracker.

□   Do one self-care activity.

□   Treat yourself with one small reward.

□   Check in with your accountability partner.

Day three of week three

□   Write for one hour or produce 2,000 words.

□   Enter your word count in the word count tracker.

□   Do one self-care activity.

□   Treat yourself with one small reward.

□   Check in with your accountability partner.

Day four of week three

□   Write for one hour or produce 2,000 words.

□   Enter your word count in the word count tracker.

□   Do one self-care activity.

□   Treat yourself with one small reward.

□   Check in with your accountability partner.

Day five of week three

□   Write for one hour or produce 2,000 words.

□   Enter your word count in the word count tracker.

□   Do one self-care activity.

□   Treat yourself with one small reward.

□   Check in with your accountability partner.

Day six of week three

□   Write for one hour or produce 2,000 words.

□   Enter your word count in the word count tracker.

□   Do one self-care activity.

- ☐ Treat yourself with one small reward.
- ☐ Check in with your accountability partner.

Day seven of week three (for those not taking a Sabbath)

- ☐ Write for one hour or produce 2,000 words.
- ☐ Enter your word count in the word count tracker.
- ☐ Do one self-care activity.
- ☐ Treat yourself with this week's medium-sized reward.

Day seven for everyone:

- ☐ Check in with your accountability partner.

Your Progress

You should have at least 10,000 words at this point. This is enough for some books. If you have the majority of your outline filled in now, great. If not, it's perfectly fine. Just keep sifting that flour . . .

Week Four

This week will consist of a lot of content creation. Conduct any interviews you haven't yet done.

Day one of week four

- ☐ Write for one hour or produce 2,000 words.
- ☐ Schedule any interviews you weren't able to conduct last week.
- ☐ Do one self-care activity.
- ☐ Treat yourself with one small reward.
- ☐ Enter your word count in the word count tracker.
- ☐ Check in with your accountability partner.

Day two of week four

- ☐ Write for one hour or produce 2,000 words.
- ☐ Do one self-care activity.
- ☐ Treat yourself with one small reward.
- ☐ Enter your word count in the word count tracker.
- ☐ Check in with your accountability partner.

Day three of week four

- ☐ Write for one hour or produce 2,000 words.
- ☐ Do one self-care activity.
- ☐ Treat yourself with one small reward.
- ☐ Enter your word count in the word count tracker.
- ☐ Check in with your accountability partner.

Day four of week four

- ☐ Write for one hour or produce 2,000 words.
- ☐ Do one self-care activity.
- ☐ Enter your word count in the word count tracker.
- ☐ Treat yourself with one small reward.
- ☐ Check in with your accountability partner.

Day five of week four

- ☐ Write for one hour or produce 2,000 words.
- ☐ Enter your word count in the word count tracker.
- ☐ Do one self-care activity.
- ☐ Treat yourself with one small reward.
- ☐ Check in with your accountability partner.

Day six of week four

- ☐ Write for one hour or produce 2,000 words.
- ☐ Enter your word count in the word count tracker.
- ☐ Do one self-care activity.
- ☐ Treat yourself with one small reward.
- ☐ Check in with your accountability partner.

Day seven of week four (for those not taking a Sabbath)

- ☐ Write for one hour or produce 2,000 words.
- ☐ Do one self-care activity.
- ☐ Give yourself this week's medium-sized treat.
- ☐ Enter your word count in the word count tracker.
- ☐ Check in with your accountability partner.

Your Progress

You should have 22,000 words or more. This is enough for many books. If you have the majority of your outline filled in now, great. If not, you still have plenty of time. You're mixing your dry ingredients.

Week Five

For those who are finished filling in their outline:

- ☐ Celebrate.
- ☐ Look over the manuscript and see what might be missing. Add examples/stories and details. Incorporate material from the interviews you conducted, if you haven't already done that.
- ☐ Share your draft with the group and ask for feedback.
- ☐ Take time to read through the drafts of anyone else in the group.
- ☐ Do one self-care activity.
- ☐ Give yourself this week's medium-sized treat.

For those who are still completing their first draft:

Day one of week five

- ☐ Write for one hour or produce 2,000 words.
- ☐ Schedule any interviews you still need to conduct.
- ☐ Do one self-care activity.
- ☐ Give yourself one small reward.
- ☐ Enter your word count in the word count tracker.
- ☐ Check in with your accountability partner.

Day two of week five

- ☐ Write for one hour or produce 2,000 words.
- ☐ Do one self-care activity.
- ☐ Give yourself one small reward.
- ☐ Enter your word count in the word count tracker.
- ☐ Check in with your accountability partner.

Day three of week five

- ☐ Write for one hour or produce 2,000 words.
- ☐ Do one self-care activity.
- ☐ Give yourself one small reward.
- ☐ Enter your word count in the word count tracker.
- ☐ Check in with your accountability partner.

Day four of week five

- ☐ Write for one hour or produce 2,000 words.
- ☐ Do one self-care activity.
- ☐ Give yourself one small reward.
- ☐ Enter your word count in the word count tracker.
- ☐ Check in with your accountability partner.

Day five of week five

- ☐ Write for one hour or produce 2,000 words.
- ☐ Do one self-care activity.
- ☐ Give yourself one small reward.
- ☐ Enter your word count in the word count tracker.
- ☐ Check in with your accountability partner.

Day six of week five

- ☐ Write for one hour or produce 2,000 words.
- ☐ Do one self-care activity.
- ☐ Give yourself one small reward.
- ☐ Enter your word count in the word count tracker.
- ☐ Check in with your accountability partner.

Day seven of week five (for those not taking a Sabbath)

- ☐ Write for one hour or produce 2,000 words.
- ☐ Do one self-care activity.
- ☐ Give yourself this week's medium-sized reward.
- ☐ Enter your word count in the word count tracker.
- ☐ Check in with your accountability partner.

Your Progress

You should have 36,000 words or more. This is enough. If you have the majority of your outline filled in now, great. If not, you still have plenty of time. Now you're beating the eggs.

Week Six

- ☐ Look over the manuscript and see what might be missing. Add examples/stories and details. It will add to your word count, but don't focus on that.
- ☐ Share your draft with the group and ask for feedback.
- ☐ Take time to read through the drafts of anyone else in the group.
- ☐ Do one self-care activity.
- ☐ Give yourself one small reward.
- ☐ Enter your word count in the word count tracker.
- ☐ Check in with your accountability partner.

Day one of week six

- ☐ Work for one hour per day or process 2,000 words.
- ☐ Do one self-care activity.
- ☐ Give yourself one small reward.
- ☐ Enter your word count in the word count tracker.
- ☐ Check in with your accountability partner.

Day two of week six

- ☐ Work for one hour per day or process 2,000 words.
- ☐ Do one self-care activity.
- ☐ Give yourself one small reward.
- ☐ Enter your word count in the word count tracker.
- ☐ Check in with your accountability partner.

Day three of week six

- ☐ Work for one hour per day or process 2,000 words.
- ☐ Do one self-care activity.
- ☐ Give yourself one small reward.

- ☐ Enter your word count in the word count tracker.
- ☐ Check in with your accountability partner.

Day four of week six

- ☐ Work for one hour per day or process 2,000 words.
- ☐ Do one self-care activity.
- ☐ Give yourself one small reward.
- ☐ Enter your word count in the word count tracker.
- ☐ Check in with your accountability partner.

Day five of week six

- ☐ Work for one hour per day or process 2,000 words.
- ☐ Do one self-care activity.
- ☐ Give yourself one small reward.
- ☐ Enter your word count in the word count tracker.
- ☐ Check in with your accountability partner.

Day six of week six

- ☐ Work for one hour per day or process 2,000 words.
- ☐ Do one self-care activity.
- ☐ Give yourself one small reward.
- ☐ Enter your word count in the word count tracker.
- ☐ Check in with your accountability partner.

Day seven of week six (for those not taking a Sabbath)

- ☐ Work for one hour per day or process 2,000 words.
- ☐ Do one self-care activity.
- ☐ Give yourself this week's medium-sized treat.
- ☐ Enter your word count in the word count tracker.
- ☐ Check in with your accountability partner.

Your Progress

You've added stories and examples. You may have 50,000 words. Stop. This is enough for nearly all nonfiction books. It's time to combine the wet and dry ingredients.

Week Seven

- ☐ Look over the manuscript again. Is every statement true and supported? Are sources cited? Is everything clear? Determine what there might be too much of. Is material repeated unnecessarily?

- ☐ Read your manuscript aloud. You'll catch a lot of errors and unclear sentences this way.

- ☐ Share your draft with someone you trust and ask for feedback.

Day one of week seven

- ☐ If you have added any material to your book, enter your word count in the word count tracker.

- ☐ Do one self-care activity.

- ☐ Give yourself one small reward.

- ☐ Check in with your accountability partner.

Day two of week seven

- ☐ If you have added any material to your book, enter your word count in the word count tracker.

- ☐ Do one self-care activity.

- ☐ Give yourself one small reward.

- ☐ Check in with your accountability partner.

Day three of week seven

- ☐ If you have added any material to your book, enter your word count in the word count tracker.

- ☐ Practice self-care.

- ☐ Give yourself one small reward.

- ☐ Check in with your accountability partner.

Day four of week seven

- ☐ If you have added any material to your book, enter your word count in the word count tracker.

- ☐ Do one self-care activity.

- ☐ Give yourself one small reward.

- ☐ Check in with your accountability partner.

Day five of week seven

- ☐ If you have added any material to your book, enter your word count in the word count tracker.
- ☐ Do one self-care activity.
- ☐ Give yourself one small reward.
- ☐ Check in with your accountability partner.

Day six of week seven

- ☐ If you have added any material to your book, enter your word count in the word count tracker.
- ☐ Practice self-care.
- ☐ Give yourself one small reward.
- ☐ Check in with your accountability partner.

Day seven of week seven

- ☐ If you have added any material to your book, enter your word count in the word count tracker.
- ☐ Do one self-care activity.
- ☐ Give yourself this week's medium-sized goody.
- ☐ Check in with your accountability partner.

Your Progress

You have a full draft, and into the oven it goes.

Week Eight

- ☐ Revise your draft, with attention to pet phrases and words that are used too often. Every writer has some of these crutches, and readers will pick up on and become annoyed by them.
- ☐ If you have added any material to your book, enter your word count in the word count tracker.

I've assigned the chapter revision based on a book with ten chapters. Adjust accordingly.

Day one of week eight

- ☐ Revise chapter one and six.

- ☐ Do one self-care activity.
- ☐ Give yourself one small reward.
- ☐ Check in with your accountability partner.

Day two of week eight

- ☐ Revise chapter two and seven.
- ☐ Do one self-care activity.
- ☐ Give yourself one small reward.
- ☐ Check in with your accountability partner.

Day three of week eight

- ☐ Revise chapter three and eight.
- ☐ Do one self-care activity.
- ☐ Give yourself one small reward.
- ☐ Check in with your accountability partner.

Day four of week eight

- ☐ Revise chapter four and nine.
- ☐ Do one self-care activity.
- ☐ Give yourself one small reward.
- ☐ Check in with your accountability partner.

Day five of week eight

- ☐ Revise chapter five and ten.
- ☐ Do one self-care activity.
- ☐ Give yourself one small reward.
- ☐ Check in with your accountability partner.

Day six of week eight

- ☐ Let your manuscript rest.
- ☐ Do one self-care activity.
- ☐ Give yourself one small reward.
- ☐ Check in with your accountability partner.

Day seven of week eight

- ☐ Let your manuscript rest.
- ☐ Do one self-care activity.

- ☐ Give yourself this week's medium-sized reward.
- ☐ Check in with your accountability partner.

Your Progress

And now it bakes . . .

Week Nine

- ☐ Revise your draft, with attention to sentence length and structure. Is there a variety? Having too many long sentences in a row tires readers. Too many short sentences frustrate readers. Vary the length. It's not necessary to follow any particular pattern. Use some simple, some compound, some complex, and some compound-complex sentences.
- ☐ If you have added any material to your book, enter your word count in the word count tracker.

Day one of week nine

- ☐ Revise chapters one and ten.
- ☐ Do one self-care activity.
- ☐ Give yourself one small reward.
- ☐ Check in with your accountability partner.

Day two of week nine

- ☐ Revise chapters two and nine.
- ☐ Do one self-care activity.
- ☐ Give yourself one small reward.
- ☐ Check in with your accountability partner.

Day three of week nine

- ☐ Revise chapters three and eight.
- ☐ Do one self-care activity.
- ☐ Give yourself one small reward.
- ☐ Check in with your accountability partner.

Day four of week nine

- ☐ Revise chapters four and seven.
- ☐ Do one self-care activity.

☐ Give yourself one small reward.

☐ Check in with your accountability partner.

Day five of week nine

☐ Revise chapters five and six.

☐ Do one self-care activity.

☐ Give yourself one small reward.

☐ Check in with your accountability partner.

Day six of week nine

☐ Let your manuscript rest.

☐ Do one self-care activity.

☐ Give yourself one small reward.

☐ Check in with your accountability partner.

Day seven of week nine

☐ Let your manuscript rest.

☐ Do one self-care activity.

☐ Give yourself this week's medium-sized treat.

☐ Check in with your accountability partner.

Week Ten

☐ Seek endorsements for your book.

☐ Write/Compile your Front Matter.

☐ If you have added any material to your book, enter your word count in the word count tracker.

Day one of week ten

☐ Write your Dedication.

☐ Do one self-care activity.

☐ Give yourself one small reward.

☐ Check in with your accountability partner.

Day two of week ten

☐ Write your Introduction if you're including one. (Few people read them.)

- ☐ Do one self-care activity.
- ☐ Give yourself one small reward.
- ☐ Check in with your accountability partner.

Day three of week ten

- ☐ Write your Copyright page. See HarshmanServices.com/YBB-book-goodies for a template.
- ☐ Do one self-care activity.
- ☐ Give yourself one small reward.
- ☐ Check in with your accountability partner.

Day four of week ten

- ☐ Do one self-care activity.
- ☐ Give yourself one small reward.
- ☐ Check in with your accountability partner.

Day five of week ten

- ☐ Do one self-care activity.
- ☐ Give yourself one small reward.
- ☐ Check in with your accountability partner.

Day six of week ten

- ☐ Do one self-care activity.
- ☐ Give yourself one small reward.
- ☐ Check in with your accountability partner.

Day seven of week ten

- ☐ Do one self-care activity.
- ☐ Give yourself this week's medium-sized reward.
- ☐ Check in with your accountability partner.

Week Eleven

- ☐ Finalize your first draft.
- ☐ Obtain your endorsements, and enter them into your manuscript.
- ☐ If you have added any material to your book, enter your word count in the word count tracker.

Day one of week eleven

☐ Do one self-care activity.

☐ Give yourself one small reward.

☐ Check in with your accountability partner.

Day two of week eleven

☐ Do one self-care activity.

☐ Give yourself one small reward.

☐ Check in with your accountability partner.

Day three of week eleven

☐ Do one self-care activity.

☐ Give yourself one small reward.

☐ Check in with your accountability partner.

Day four of week eleven

☐ Do one self-care activity.

☐ Give yourself one small reward.

☐ Check in with your accountability partner.

Day five of week eleven

☐ Do one self-care activity.

☐ Give yourself one small reward.

☐ Check in with your accountability partner.

Day six of week eleven

☐ Do one self-care activity.

☐ Give yourself one small reward.

☐ Check in with your accountability partner.

Day seven of week eleven

☐ Do one self-care activity.

☐ Give yourself this week's medium-sized reward.

☐ Check in with your accountability partner.

You are so close to finishing this stage of the book-writing process. I want you to look back at how far you've come, and celebrate it. You deserve it!

Week Twelve

Write your Back Matter this week.

Day one of week twelve

- ☐ Write your Acknowledgments page.
- ☐ Do one self-care activity.
- ☐ Give yourself one small reward.
- ☐ Check in with your accountability partner.

Day two of week twelve

- ☐ Write your Resources page.
- ☐ Do one self-care activity.
- ☐ Give yourself one small reward.
- ☐ Check in with your accountability partner.

Day three of week twelve

- ☐ Do one self-care activity.
- ☐ Give yourself one small reward.
- ☐ Check in with your accountability partner.

Day four of week twelve

- ☐ Do one self-care activity.
- ☐ Give yourself one small reward.
- ☐ Check in with your accountability partner.

Day five of week twelve

- ☐ Do one self-care activity.
- ☐ Give yourself one small reward.
- ☐ Check in with your accountability partner.

Day six of week twelve

- ☐ Do one self-care activity.
- ☐ Give yourself one small reward.
- ☐ Check in with your accountability partner.

Day seven of week twelve

- ☐ Give yourself this week's medium-sized goody.

Your Progress

Now that your book has been baked, let it cool. Next, have it shaped (edited). Then have it frosted (have a cover created for it and the interior designed).

After that, you'll want to display it (do all of the after-draft marketing tasks). Most authors struggle with this. No one can do every one of the possible book-marketing tasks. It's important to choose a few of them and do them well.

Cut out the following page if you'd like, and use it as motivation. You may also download the full-color version on the website.

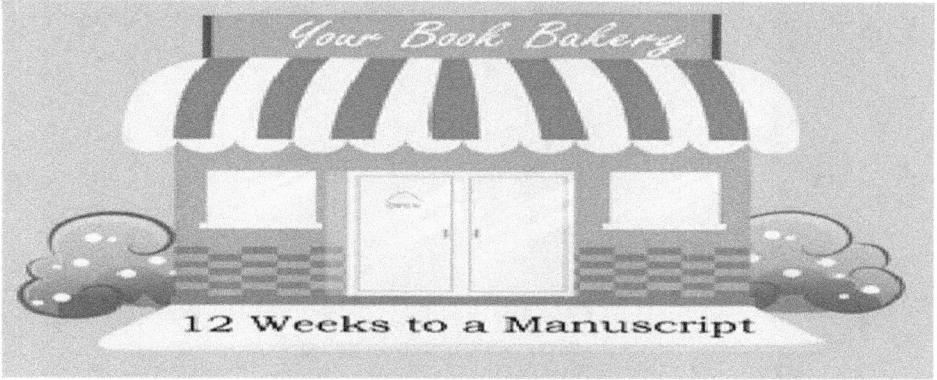

Congratulations on having completed your draft!

Celebrate!

Now, let your manuscript rest for a while. Give it a month or so before you open it again.

Then revise it. Be ruthless. Slice it up. Examine it.

Does the order of your book still make sense? Have you decided some things need to be rearranged or removed?

Move on to the next steps. Engage an agency and ask them to evaluate your manuscript and give you a quote for everything it needs. Decide if you want to work with them, and budget for what your book needs.

If You Need Help with the Writing

Even with the best recipes, intentions, and efforts, plenty of people find that they don't want to write their book alone. Maybe they need some company. Perhaps they want more support than a book can give.

If any of that applies to you, then you're welcome to join us in Your Book Bakery. There, we walk you through the process with as much or as little support as you'd like.

Most people need help writing their book. There's nothing wrong with that!

If all of this seems daunting even after seeing it broken down into steps with a recipe to follow, just reach out to me. The program called Your Book Bakery is affordable, and it covers all of this, with live Q&A and ongoing support for as long as you need to bake your book.

And no matter what, remember that you can do this. If you make it fun, it will get done!

Resources

This is one of my favorite parts of a book. Because things change so rapidly now, I've put most of this section on my website so it can be updated as needed.

Go to www.HarshmanServices.com/YBB-book-goodies

Parts of a Book

Below are the parts of a book along with explanations of what they are and whether each is required or optional.

Please note: we are happy to edit anything written in connection with our client's books. This includes all of these parts as well as any blog posts, press releases, and other pieces.

Front Matter

This is the list of the parts. For the terms that need explanation, the description is below. Some of these have lowercase Roman numerals.

Half title page. Optional.

Series title, other works, frontispiece, endorsements, or blank.

Title page. Required.

Copyright page. Required.

Dedication. Optional.

Epigraph. Optional.

Table of Contents. Required.

List of illustrations. Optional.

List of tables. Optional.

Foreword. Optional.

Preface. Optional.

Acknowledgments. Optional. (For books on Amazon, this is usually moved to the end of the book now.)

Introduction. Optional.

Body (of the book)

Main part of the book. Page numbering starts to use Arabic numerals (1,2,3, etc.) Required.

Epilogue or Afterword. Optional.

Back Matter

Acknowledgments (if not in Front Matter). Optional.

Appendix. Discouraged unless absolutely necessary.

Abbreviations used (if not in Front Matter). Optional.

Glossary. Optional.

Endnotes. Optional.

Resources. Optional.

About the Author. Optional but strongly recommended.

Mind Mapping Template

This is available for download at Harshman Services:

https://www.harshmanservices.com/free-mind-map-starter-sheet/

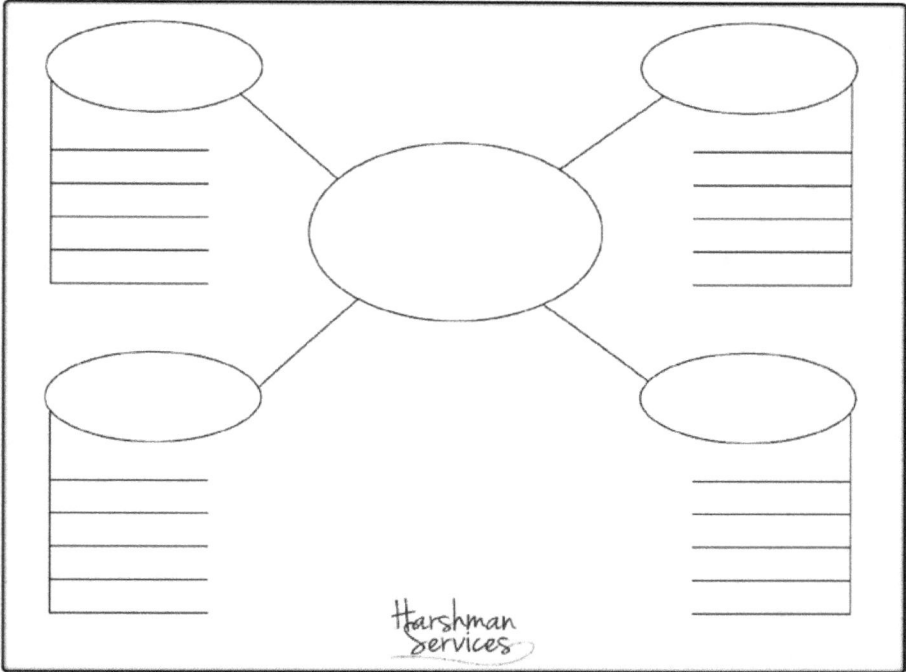

Progress Chart

Chart your progress here. Mark every day you do the work. Visit www.harshmanservices.com/YBB-book-goodies to get a printable version and find stickers that work well with this chart.

Chart your progress here. Mark every day you do the work.

Week 1							
Week 2							
Week 3							
Week 4							
Week 5							
Week 6							
Week 7							
Week 8							
Week 9							
Week 10							
Week 11							
Week 12							

Template For Writing a Book

Get a downloadable copy of our book writing template at www.harshmanservices.com/book-template Omit the headings that are centered below. They are only here to tell you which part of the book the items that follow the headings go in. Replace the words that are *in this font* with the actual content that needs to go there. For the items with this font, title the pages with those labels, and add the content that needs to go on them.

Front Matter

Title page

Copyright page

Dedication

Table of Contents

    Chapter 1: (Title)

    Chapter 2: (Title)

    Chapter 3: (Title)

    Chapter 4: (Title)

    Chapter 5: (Title)

    Chapter 6: (Title)

    Chapter 7: (Title)

    Chapter 8: (Title)

    Chapter 9: (Title)

    Chapter 10: (Title)

Foreword (Someone other than the author writes this.)

Preface

Introduction

Body (of the book)

Chapter 1: (Title)

Chapter 2: (Title)

Chapter 3: (Title)

Back Matter

Writing and Publishing Checklist

The amount of time something takes depends on several factors. Here are some:

- the length of your book
- the team member's schedule and capacity
- the amount of work that needs to be done
- how much time you have to work on it during the times it's with you
- how quickly you progress in that work

Your editor or agency owner should give you some ballpark timelines so that you have some idea of what to expect. Please be flexible and patient regarding the target dates. Communicate if you're going to be late for any reason. Your service providers should do the same.

☐ Develop a website for your book. I recommend Site Build It for their robust and easy to use tools.

☐ Create your lead magnets.

- [ ] Build a mailing list with an autoresponder such as ConvertKit. Upload your lead magnet. Begin emailing your subscribers on a weekly basis. Update them on your progress. Ask them questions to get their buy-in, and so on.

- [ ] Start marketing your book, and continue until you die or decide to remove it from the market. After every step that's listed here, mentally add, "Keep marketing."

- [ ] Consider whether to repurpose content to make it part of your book.

- [ ] Write the book. As you do, post on social media at least a few times a week.

- [ ] Practice self-care.

- [ ] If you have not done so, set up social media accounts. There are hundreds of social media platforms. Here are a few of the most popular: TikTok, Facebook, LinkedIn, Instagram, and Pinterest.

- [ ] Let your manuscript rest.

- [ ] Revise it.

- [ ] Practice self-care.

- [ ] Send the manuscript to the developmental editor.

- [ ] Make your revisions, making sure to practice self-care.

- [ ] Send it back to the developmental editor.

- [ ] Take a week off.

- [ ] Write your author bio, dedication, Acknowlegments, and any other Front or Back Matter.

- [ ] When your manuscript comes back, add those elements, and send it to a copy editor.

- [ ] Accept the changes, and talk to the editor about any changes you don't understand.

- [ ] Write the book cover copy and other blurbs.

- [ ] Build your advanced reader team (ART) or street team. Give them requirements that will help your book be successful. Tell them you'll send their advance reader copies (ARCs) when they are ready.

☐ Decide on which people you'd like to endorse your book, and send the manuscript to them and your ART.

☐ Fix any problems they point out.

☐ Obtain your endorsements.

☐ Send it back to your copy editor for a quick check of your changes and insertion of endorsements.

☐ Obtain an ISBN through Bowker or your agency.

☐ Next is the interior design and layout. Several different tools exist.

- Canva (Don't do it; it's a trick.)
- Microsoft Word (It's designed for writing, not formatting.)
- InDesign (This is the current standard used by professionals.)

☐ Create a design element list for the interior, and send it to the interior designer.

☐ Review and finalize designed pages.

☐ Send ARCs to your ART. Give them the agreed-upon time to read it and respond to you.

☐ Proofread the book, and send any needed changes to the formatter.

☐ Set the cover price for your book. If you sell on Amazon, the price you set determines the percentage you'll be paid on each sale. Choose wisely.

☐ Your book needs a cover. Unless you have a degree in design or have been paid to create book covers, please leave this one to the pros.

☐ So, write a creative brief for your cover design, and let your designer do the work.

☐ Review and finalize the cover.

☐ Decide between offset printing and Print-On-Demand (POD). If you choose offset printing, talk with the printer about costs, print runs, distribution, and delivery dates. If you choose POD, such as Amazon, there's no need to do that.

☐ Select a publication date and inform your ART of it and remind them of their responsibilities.

- ☐ Open an Amazon Author account if you don't already have one.
- ☐ Create your Amazon Author page.
- ☐ Upload your book to Amazon, including selecting categories and keywords for your book.
- ☐ Order proof copies 21 days before your publication date. During that time, continue to market your book, but otherwise, rest.
- ☐ Review the proof copies, locate remaining errors (every published book has some). Send changes to the formatter.
- ☐ Send thank-you gifts to your beta readers, ARC readers, and ART.
- ☐ Reupload your corrected files.
- ☐ Upload the files to other platforms/outlets.
- ☐ Have your formatter create e-book files.
- ☐ Upload the e-book version to all of your chosen platforms/outlets.
- ☐ Email your list to get sales.
- ☐ Publish and party.
- ☐ Register your copyright with the US Copyright Office if desired (many self-publishers skip this).
- ☐ Learn all of the requirements and specification for audiobooks.
- ☐ Purchase needed equipment or hire a voiceover actor or audiobook reader.
- ☐ Begin audiobook production.
- ☐ Review audio files.
- ☐ Polish audio files.
- ☐ Upload audiobook.
- ☐ Email your list to get sales.
- ☐ Build sales funnels for your current and backlist titles.
- ☐ Continue marketing your book.

- ☐ Repurpose your book's content. Use it to point potential readers to your book.

- ☐ If doing so serves your business, after a time, begin research for your next book and start the process all over again. Each book sells your other books, and every book helps to open doors for you as well as serving the readers.

If you're too busy to do all of this on your own, or if this 70-step list makes you feel overwhelmed, it's 100% okay. We help people through this process every day.

If you want help, just email Jennifer@HarshmanServices.com. We'll see if we're a good fit for each other regarding these stages of your project. Regardless, sign up to receive our free emails. They walk you through parts of the process and tell you about helpful resources along the way.

Ghostwriter Directory

If you need more help getting your book written than a book, course, or coaching program can provide, then you'll want a ghostwriter. On the following pages are some. See which ones you think might be worth contacting, and go for it.

Pricing Info:

Price range: $ (Under $25,000)
Price range: $$ (Between $25,000 and $50,000)
Price range: $$$ (Between $50,000 and $75,000)
Price range: $$$$ (Between $75,000 and $100,000)
Price range: $$$$$ ($100,000 or more)

April Tribe Giauque

641 Fillmore
St Twin Falls, ID 83301

Phone: 801-719-8662

Email: april@apriltribe.com

Website: www.apriltribegiauque.com

April is a ghostwriter, editor, amplifying speaker, and podcaster. She is also a victor over domestic violence and walks a healing journey. She can help you bring your story to light, and income, impact, and influence are the result.

"I help sur-thriver authors experience a victory voice in their book, and a mindset changed with my ghostwriting that impacts the world. My experience and storytelling are key factors in hooking in your readers. As a mom of nine children, I have learned a thing or two about love and life. The energy I bring to the ghostwriting process will be like nothing you have ever experienced. Let's shine!"

Specialties: memoir, self-help, business writing

Books written as of 2022: more than a dozen

Price range: $ (Under $25,000)

Andrew Wood, PhD

1111 Carriage Road
Papillion, NE 68046

Phone: 402-889-3750

Email:
andrew@copycatbusinesswriting.com

Website: copycatbusinesswriting.com

Andrew has his doctorate and spent 20 years teaching undergraduates cross-cultural communication, history, and world religions. He has lived abroad and traveled to over 25 countries. He loves explaining complex subjects in a way that is accessible to a general audience. Andrew is married, has three grown children, and is equally a dog- and cat person (with guinea pigs as a bonus!)

With his broad background, research experience, and intellectual curiosity, Andrew feels comfortable writing on a wide range of topics. He has previously edited five books in religious studies; has ghostwritten books on post-traumatic growth, Social Security, and building a social media influencing business; and has written client blogs on current movies, new business startups, and technology. He has extensive experience in Christian writing but appreciates and works sensitively with people of all worldviews. Andrew's emphasis is on helping the client communicate their message clearly and compellingly—as trouble-free as possible.

Price range: $ (Under $25,000)

Mike Loomis

Email: mike@mikeloomis.co

Website: https://mikeloomis.co/

Mike Loomis helps people launch their dream books, brands, and businesses. The author of *Your Brand Is Calling* and *My Book Launch Planner*, he's a strategic partner to bestselling authors, non-profits, publishers as well as startups, and aspiring messengers. Mike and his wife live in the mountains of Colorado with their pet moose.

Specialties: self-help, memoirs, business, faith, and government policy

Books written as of 2022: nearly three dozen

Price range: $$ (Between $25,000 and $50,000)

Kent Sanders
Inkwell Ghostwriting
783 Bear Mountain Dr.
St. Peters MO 63376
Phone: (636) 541-8231

Email:
kent@inkwellghostwriting.com

Kent Sanders is the founder of Inkwell Ghostwriting, which helps leaders grow their business through books and other content. He is also the author and coauthor of numerous books, including *18 Words to Live By: A Father's Wisdom on What Matters Most* and coauthor of *The Faith of Elvis: A Story Only a Brother Can Tell* with Billy Stanley, Elvis Presley's stepbrother. In addition, Kent is the host of *The Daily Writer* podcast and the founder of the Daily Writer Club, a membership community that helps writers build a business with their skills.

"When we work together, we don't just create a book with information. We design a book that helps advance your business and personal goals. A book is one of the best investments you will ever make for your life and business!"

Specialties: personal development, inspirational, memoir, and business. Examples include *The Faith of Elvis* (memoir) and *Performance Driven Giving* (business)

Books written as of 2022: nearly a dozen

Price range: $$$ (Between $50,000 and $75,000)

Jim Woods

2725 Valley Rd
Cuyahoga Falls, OH 44223

Phone: 615-390-8908

Email: jimwoodswrites@gmail.com

Jim Woods helps others with nonfiction books about productivity, business, mental health, entrepreneurship, and marketing. These books encourage and show readers ways to change their lives in positive way.

Jim says, "If you have a story to tell, I believe you must share it with the world. But that's hard to do own your own. I would be honored to help you bring that story into the world."

Specialty: repurposing existing content and turning it into a book. If you have a course, podcast, or blog, Jim would love to help you reshape that content into a book. Creating a book like *The War of Art* by Steven Pressfield, *Poke The Box* by Seth Godin, or *Tools of Titans* by Tim Ferriss (in 130–200 pages, not 700 pages) are right in his wheelhouse.

Books written as of 2022: half a dozen

Price range: $ (Under $25,000) to $$$ (up to $75,000)

Kay Helm

PO Box 2477

Williamsburg, VA 23187

(804) 505-4929

https://kayhelm.com

social: @ kayhelm

host: Life and Mission Podcast

Kay helps missionaries, organizations, and leaders tell powerful and effective stories that inspire action.

Specialties: fundraising, nonprofits, marketing, strategy, faith (Christian), business, international development

Books written as of 2022: 1/4 of a dozen

Price range: $$ (Between $25,000 and $50,000)

Harshman Services

Harshman Services has a team of ghostwriters on staff, with years of experience and the following specialties:

Nonfiction

Business	Personal development
Education	Parenting
Energy industry	Pet care
Entrepreneurship	Psychology
History	Self-Help
Memoir	Workbooks/Journals

Fiction

Action/Adventure	Cozy mysteries
Children's books	Historical fiction
Clean/Inspirational romance	Political thrillers

Books written as of 2022: dozens

Price range: $ (Under $25,000) to $$$$ (up to $100,000)

Contact us for a custom quote.

Acknowledgments

If you are reading this, then you are in this book's Acknowledgments section—and deserve to be. Why? Because *you are the reason I wrote this book*.

You want to make a difference in this world, and that is what this book (and every book I write) is all about. If you have the right attitudes and the right resources, you can do amazing things; if you will choose the first, you will find the second. You found this book, and you're using it. Way to go!

It's easy to think that someone would know if they contributed to a book. And that thanking them in the Acknowledgments section is not to inform them but to showcase them. One might also think that an author could simply contact each person to say thank you. It's not always the case with any of those things.

Sometimes, a person contributes to a book without knowing it. Often, it's in a positive way. It's not unheard of for someone to provide examples of what *not* to do, and those are necessary and helpful, too. If an author really considers the situation, something will become clear. Many of the people who contributed in some way to the book are people the author can't easily reach to thank. Doing it in this section of their book is something they *can* do.

Here are some others who deserve recognition:

Aaron Hunt	Alana Sheldahl
Abigail Wild	Alexander Harshman
Abingdon Press	Alice Sullivan
Adam McCarty	Allan Dubon
Adam Zach	Amanda Kelly
Aisha Winfield	Amy Elizabeth Harrill
Alan Harshman	Ancient Faith Publishing

Andrea Hollander

Andy Storch

Andy Traub

Angela England

Anna Powers

Anthony Woolever

Ashley Logdson

Barry Karch

Becca White

Bee Andreen

Ben Esteban

Ben Killoy

Benjamin Hardy, PhD

Bill Konves

Blake Atwood

Brad Coleman

Brad Imming

Brad Ritter

Brian J Dixon, PhD

Brian Mays

Bryan Argott

Bryan Harris

Cathy Jackson

Chad Jeffers

Charlotte Riggle

Chris Comer

Chris Hines

Chris Holmes

Chris Knighton

Chris McClure

Chris Niemeyer

Christine Hughey

Christine Odle

Christopher McCluskey

Cliff Ravenscraft

Cole James

Connie Albers

Courtney Wisely

Dan Barker

Dan Hinz

Dan Miller

Dan Speicher

Dan Sullivan

Daniel Bauer

Dave Burgess Consulting

David C. Gilmore

David Hancock

Debi Ronca

Denis Nurmela

Dennis A Clark

Derek Stone

Desha Utsick

Dick Margulis

Dirk Maierhafer

Dotty J. Young

Elaine Appleton Grant

Elissa D. Bjeletich

Elizabeth Fisco Pugliese

Emily Brunner

Engel Jones

Erik K. Johnson

Erin Casey

Gabe Arnold

Greg Gerber

Greg Tosi

Harvey Ramer

Heather Woosley

Honorée Corder

Indi Williams, PhD.

James Banker

James Woosley

Janeen Kilgore

Jannette Isaacson

Jared Easley

Jared Odle

Jason Goth

Jay Parks, CPA

J.D. Elliott

Jeff Brown

Jeff Goins

Jeff Walker

Jen Smith

Jennifer Nicole Marco

Jennifer Priest

Jerad Spencer

Jeremy Allen

Jeremy Lewis

Jim Woods

Joanna Penn

Jody Maberry

Jody Skinner

Joel Michael Harshman

John Biethan

John G. Miller

John Lee Dumas

John Schuchman

John Stange

John Vander Meulen

John Wells

Jon Appino

Jonathan Tavarez

Josh Melton

Joy Worthington Mansfield

Kachina Gosselin

Karen Anderson

Katherine Sands

Kathy Kolbe

Katlynn Pyatt

Kay Helm

Ken Carfagno

Ken Hannaman

Ken Hoops

Kent Julian

Kent Sanders

Kevin Miller

Khouria Patty Kishler

Kimanzi Constable

Kristina Michelle Roth

Lary Crews

Lauri Lechner

Lee Brower

Lee Cockerell

Lisa Russell

Lisa Thompson

Louise Harnby

Lucas Marino

Lukas Loveland

Marc Mawhinney

Marcia Ferguson

Marcus Gates

Mark Ross

Martha Peterson

Mary Valloni

Matt Peet

Melinda Tipton Martin

Melinda Walker

Melissa Bloom

Melissa Goth

Melissa Elizabeth Naasko

Melissa Etherton

Michael Hyatt

Michele Sharpe Williams

Michelle Allegrezza

Michelle King Cohen

Mike DeHaan

Mike Forrester

Mike Kim

Mike Snyder

M.J. James

My Writers Connection

Nancy Becher

Natalie Alcantara

Nick Adams

Nick Elkins

Nick Loper

Nick Pavlidis

Nikole Potulsky

Noël Joy Plourde

Pantea Vahidi

Park End Books

Pat Flynn

Paul Joy

Paul Thompson

Peter Shankman

Phil Mershon

Phil Pavely

Philipp Lomboy

Phillip Carson, M.D.

Phyllis Jenkins

Rachel Richards

Rebecca Harshman

Rebecca Patrick-Howard

Rebekah Hughes

Reina Rose

Renee Vidor

Rick Blodgett

Robert David Orr

Rocky Buckley

Rocky Lalvani

Ron Price

Ron Skillens

Ryan Fairbanks

Rye Taylor

Samuel Oshunbun

Sandra Hill

Scott Johnson

Seth Godin	Thomas McGreevy
Shā Sparks	Tim Sample
Shawn Washburn	Tina Marie Morlock
Shayla Lee Raquel	Tommy Breedlove
Shylla Webb	Tracy Davison
Sonya McCllough Lockridge	Tricia Verst Prues
Steve Robinson	Troy Stoneking
Summer Kinard	Victoria Mininger
Tad Dickel, PhD.	Victoria Vane
Tammy Foster	Vincent Pugliese
Teresa McCloy	Wendy Norman
Terry Stafford	Winston Faircloth
Theresa Winn	Yvette Davis
Thomas DeVore	Yvette Marie

A therapist who volunteered at the free clinic in Kansas City introduced me to art therapy sometime around 2005. She said she knew that someday she'd be reading my books and watching my career blossom.

To her, I say this: within a few years of receiving your encouragement, I achieved everything we talked about and more. I created a life I love, helping people make a difference in this world, and I am grateful every single day. Thank you for making a difference.

www.ingramcontent.com/pod-product-compliance
Lightning Source LLC
LaVergne TN
LVHW052022080426
835513LV00018B/2111